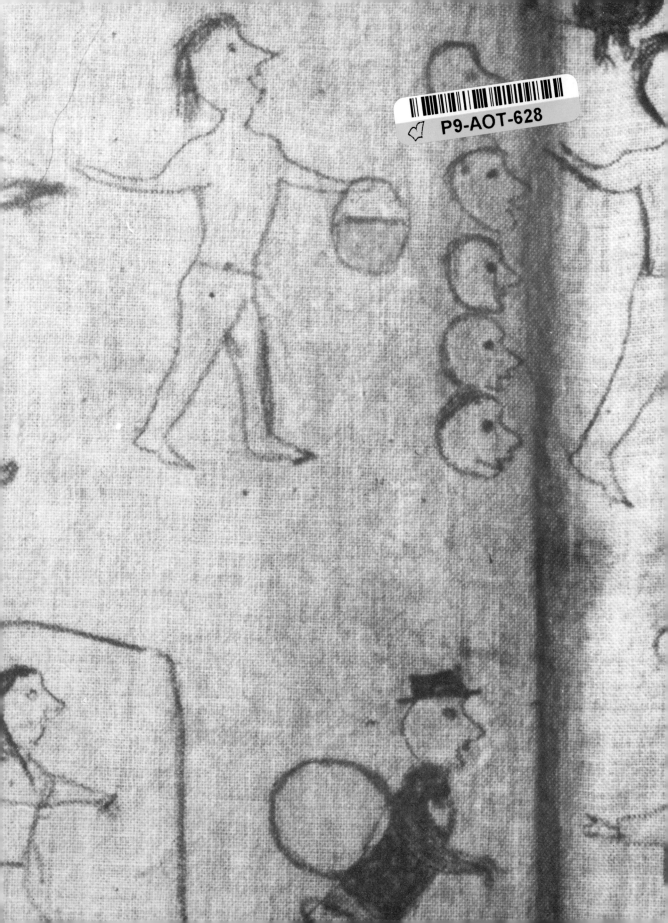

THE WHITE MEN

THE

Times
BOOKS

WHITE MEN

The first response of aboriginal peoples to the white man

JULIA BLACKBURN

Foreword by
Dr Edmund Carpenter

First published by Orbis Publishing Ltd, London 1979

© 1979 by Julia Blackburn

Printed in England by
Hazell Watson and Viney Ltd

Library of Congress Cataloging in Publication Data

Blackburn, Julia.
The White Men

Bibliography: p.
Includes index.

1. Man, Primitive – First contact with Occidental civilization.   I. Title.
GN368.B57   1979   301.29   79–9859
ISBN 0–8129–0826–0

ENDPAPERS: Some of the Plains Indians kept 'winter counts', a pictographic calendar of their history. This one was drawn on to a cotton cloth by a Yanktonai Sioux called Blue Thunder. It records events which took place between 1792–3 and 1902–3.

FULL-TITLE: The rail on a Kasai chieftain's chair shows a seated white European officer being carried by his Congolese soldiers.

THE PUBLISHERS WOULD LIKE TO ACKNOWLEDGE THE HELP OF THE FOLLOWING MUSEUMS, PRIVATE COLLECTIONS AND INDIVIDUALS IN PERMITTING THE REPRODUCTION OF THE PHOTOGRAPHY SHOWN ON THE PAGES LISTED:

Efriam Andersson: page 175. David Attenborough: pages 79, 84. Auckland Institute and Museum: page 144. Julia Blackburn: pages 182, 183. Brighton Pavilion Museum: pages 114, 171. By courtesy of the Trustees of the British Museum: pages 14, 27, 32, 39, 43, 47, 51, 55, 63, 67, 167. Professor Herbert M. Cole: pages 12, 13, 89. Mike Dye: pages 14, 15R, 19, 22, 23, 38, 39, 51, 54, 59, 63, 87, 114, 151. Werner Forman Archive: pages 11, 27, 32, 43, 47, 55, 67, 90, 93, 108, 111, 135. Philip Goldman Collection: page 151. Haddon Collection, Cambridge University Museum of Archaeology and Ethnology: pages 16–17, 52, 91, 95, 96, 162. Joslyn Art Museum, Omaha, Nebraska: page 90. Koninklijk Museum voor Midden-Africa, Tevuren: pages 15R, 19, 22, 23, 38, 53T, 53B, 54, 59, 61, 87, 142. Merseyside County Museum, Liverpool: pages 98–99. Musée de l'Homme, Paris: pages 28, 29, 36, 40. Museum of the American Indian, New York: pages 131, 179. Museum F. Volkerkunde, Vienna: pages 21, 125. Museum Volkerkunde, Freiburg in Breisgau: page 119. National Museum, Copenhagen: pages 146–7. John Picton: page 153. Pitt Rivers Museum, Oxford: pages 75, 103. Axel Poignant: pages 34, 69. Rautenstrauch-Joest Museum, Cologne: page 15L. Rijksmuseum voor Volkenkunde, Leiden: page 20. The Royal Anthropological Institute: pages 56, 100. J.S. Slotkin: page 160. Smithsonian Institution, Washington: pages 24, 126, 128, 133, 135, 138, 139, 154. Dorota Starzecka: page 167. Andrew Strathern: pages 48, 81. Joan Westcott: pages 121, 165. H.C. Woodhouse: pages 31, 107, 122.

Many people helped in the preparation of this book, but the author would like to offer her special thanks to John Picton, Werner Forman, Andrew Strathern and the staff of the Royal Anthropological Institute Library.

CONTENTS

Foreword   6

Introduction   10

The White Men Arrive   26

White Man's Secrets   50

The Races of Man   86

The Land of the Dead   118

The Aftermath   150

Tribal Locations   184
Notes   187
Acknowledgments   188
Bibliography   190
Index   191

FOREWORD

In the fascinating text of this book, Julia Blackburn has compiled many first responses – at once both educational and entertaining – which present illuminating interpretations of the white people by aboriginal peoples. I wonder if there ever existed in the world, at least in recent centuries, a tribe so isolated that they have no memory of other peoples? John Ross, in *An Account of the Discovery of the Polar Eskimo* (1819), tells of meeting these northern-most peoples:

> They first pointed to the ships, eagerly asking, what great creatures those were. Do they come from the sun or the moon? Do they give us light by night or by day? Sacheuse [a southern Eskimo interpreter] told them that he was a man, that he had a father and a mother like themselves; and pointing to the south, said that he came from a distant country in that direction. To this they answered, 'That cannot be, there is nothing but ice there'.

But recently archaeologists discovered, in this northwestern part of Greenland, trade objects from Baffinland. This seems to throw doubt on the belief that the Polar Eskimos were really totally unaware of other peoples. I also doubt some other accounts, especially recent ones of happy bands running free and wild in their native habitats, uncontaminated by the follies and vices of civilization. These accounts are media creations.

It is romantic illusion to imagine 'We were the first that ever burst/into that silent sea'. European explorers in the South Pacific followed trade routes established a millennium or more before by traders from the ports of Asia. We hear of Samuel de Champlain exploring New France in 1610. By then, Frenchmen had fished the Grand Banks for a century; the inland Seneca, for example, had French trade goods by at least 1540. Champlain reported that he was met by musket fire. Trade goods usually preceded actual contact. When the 1935 Hides-O'Malley patrol reached the head-waters of the Erave in unexplored New Guinea, a tribesman with a steel tomahawk alternately pointed to the tomahawk and to the patrol's route home.

And stories usually preceded contact. Even Herodotus, writing about 430 BC, mixed fact and fancy about north Europeans:

> But of the land on the other side of the bald man, none can give any trustworthy account because it is shut off by a separating wall of lofty trackless mountains, which no man can cross. But these bald men say – which, however, I do not believe – that men with goat's feet live in the mountains, and on the other side of them men who sleep six months at a time.... The whole of the country which I have been speaking of has so hard and severe winter, that there prevails there for eight months an altogether unsupportable cold ... even the sea freezes.[1]

When ever people meet the unfamiliar, they at once translate it into something they already know, and that means they never face the unfamiliar directly.

> The Kwakiuti Indian, whom [the anthropologist] Boas sometimes invited to New York to serve him as an informant, was indifferent to the spectacle of skyscrapers and streets lined with automobiles. He reserved all his intellectual curiosity for the dwarfs, giants, and bearded ladies which were at that time exhibited in Times Square, for automats, and the brass balls decorating staircase bannisters . . . all these things challenged his own culture, and it was that culture alone he was seeking to recognize in certain aspects of ours.[2]

Most tribal peoples lack the kind of conceptual tools for experiencing the unknown. In contrast to them, Western man has a long tradition of dealing with the alien. Mediterranean traders and European explorers labelled and classified everything they encountered, no matter how extraordinary. They had money and numbers which helped immeasurably in trade and translation, and they had three-dimensional perspective in art by which even the strangest bird or flower could be optically rendered.

Tribal artists had no such means. Compare these two portraits of a Maori chieftain, Tupa Kupa: the first (left) by an Englishman, the second (right) by himself.[3] Each employs a learned art form, but the Maori's drawing is more symbol than likeness, whereas the Englishman's drawing matches nature: the viewer sees what he would have seen had he been there, and thus, the not-knower becomes the knower.

I once exchanged portraits with a Papuan. Using three-dimensional perspective, I created an optical likeness of him that his fellow tribesman could recognize as his portrait. His portrait of me, however, was not individually identifiable. Since I was a white stranger, he saw me as a ghost and he painted me as a headless, reptile-like figure, which is the conventional Papuan motif for all ancestors. This was an ideal symbol for weaving someone into the seamless web of Papuan kinship, but to incorporate someone into Western society, you need optical likeness. Then you can classify and conquer.

Western man conquered and classified everything he could use. He put the native peoples of conquered countries to work on plantations; he recorded their customs in textbooks; and he collected their art for his own museum collections. It was largely a one-way conquest.

European languages, in particular, are highly systemized, whereas preliterate languages, though every bit as sophisticated as European ones, are designed to reaffirm the known, not to explore. Thus the Eskimo has about two dozen separate words for different types of snow, but no single word meaning snow. By contrast, the mass nouns and modifiers of standard Indo-European languages enable a speaker to describe whatever he observes, no matter how alien.

When first exposed to European culture, what did most natives 'see'? I suspect most *saw* very little. Since an object cannot be seen apart from its interpretation, where there was no interpretation, probably there was no perception. It was a favourite trick in the sixteenth century to invite unsuspecting natives aboard a galleon, then discharge a cannon. Repeatedly we are told that the visitors did not react: they appeared *not to have heard*. Later, they learned to flee.

But even after fleeing, how did they describe what they had heard? Even if they had possessed words in their vocabularies to describe that sound – which they did not – they had no tradition of 'foreign news'. A preliterate storyteller generally assumes everyone shares his knowledge. So he ignores or alters cause and effect, and tells stories which often begin with the crisis, so to speak, then weave backwards and forwards in time, with many omissions and repetitions, always on the assumption that the listener's mind moves in the same groove as the storyteller's and that no elucidation is necessary. This can make for great storytelling, but only if each listener already knows every detail.

Do we ever really know how natives see us? We seldom ask. No one asked Friday his opinion about Robinson Crusoe, though Crusoe was obviously a very strange character. It flatters us to think that natives everywhere see us with all the wide-eyed wonder of the child, dazzled by our technology, awed by our intelligence. We love stories about our machines being mistaken for animals and our media being mistaken for gods. The truth is less flattering.

When Knud Rasmussen, the great arctic explorer (himself part Eskimo), visited the Netsilingmuit in northern Canada, he found it difficult to learn their true appraisal of any white man. Often, he felt, they regarded a white man the way white men regarded Eskimos – as inferior. But they also regarded him as a powerful barbarian: bigger, stronger and more powerfully equipped than themselves, a member of a strong nation that lived in a great distant land. Old, orthodox Eskimos, he found, regarded the white man, like Indians, as bastard offspring of an arrogant, disobedient woman and a dog. (The story of this union is told in *The Woman who mated with a Dog*.) However, all who met a white man could not help admiring him and subjecting themselves entirely to his will. They believed his resources were inexhaustible.

Whether he came by sail or sled, he always brought into this poor country an impressive wealth of implements and food. He knew how to navigate and how to determine his position by the sun. Above all, firearms made him a formidable competitor for food and a terrible enemy.

Still, Eskimos were always superior in living in this cold land, building snowhuts, driving dogs and paddling kayaks. In many ways the white man was dependent on them. But, whatever opinion one formed of him, all agreed he had to be treated with caution. These views were explained to Rasmussen by old Kuvduitsoq, who concluded:

It is generally believed white men have the same minds as children. Therefore one should always give way to them. They are easily angered, and when they cannot get their will, they are moody, and like children, have the strangest ideas and fancies.[4]

In the illuminating stories which follow, the colonizing white man is revealed through the eyes of the aboriginal peoples from Australasia, North America and Africa.

Edmund Carpenter

INTRODUCTION

The foreigner
Chin of a goat
The foreigner comes striding haughtily
With his red skin[1]
(Oral Literature in Africa by Ruth Finnegan)

THIS IS AN ANTHOLOGY of stories about the white man, told by people for whom white men were strange intruders from an unknown land. It is a collection of responses to the white man and the things that he brought with him – his goods and his gods – coming from people who had no preconceptions about Western society, and who did not even know that it existed until the moment when it burst in upon them.

Mirror images, reflections of civilization. Men, or are they gods, or are they the dead ancestors who have clambered angrily out of their graves to come and take their revenge on the living? Creatures with red faces and red hands, and no bodies visible; and why do they hide their bodies? Have they no skin under that carefully fitted and concealing cloth? The pale colour of their skin must belong to creatures who have lived under the ground, or in the sea perhaps. The pale colour of their skin is the colour of fear, of death. A child remembers how, when he was first touched by a white hand, the whiteness burnt him, making him cry out in pain.

Sometimes rumours spread from one group to the next. Sometimes it is said that they bring wonderful gifts with them, and soon there will be no more hunger and no more death. Sometimes unknown sicknesses herald their approach and whole communities are wiped out in the sudden contagion. The people are half-crazed in the expectation of miracles and disasters, and yet, in spite of all their anticipations, the arrival of the white men must shock and surprise them. They watch how they drop down out of the belly of the Great Mother Bird of the Sky, the one who has been making the earth shake with her terrible song. They see them emerging from the Big-house-ship, whose bright lights had been gleaming on the distant horizon for many nights. They run when they hear the shining, noisy animals that carry these strangers across the country. These animals leave deep scarred tracks behind them wherever they travel and the people are afraid of the tracks which do not show the print of a foot.

It is imperative to find out who the white men are, why they have come here, and what they now intend to do. Perhaps the people observe them from a safe distance, or they might boldly welcome them with gifts and feasts, or attempt to chase them away with their weapons and their

RIGHT
For a long time the power of the British Empire was represented by stylized portraits of Queen Victoria. In this conventionalized carving from the Mende people of Sierra Leone, she is given an elongated neck as a sign of beauty and her naked body is scarred with medals and other royal insignia.

magical incantations. It is not possible to ignore these new creatures who assert their presence with such immediate presumption, as if they own all the land that they have just come to, as if they are the real masters of all that they see.

White man sits in the shade and sweats. He eats his own food and he sleeps in his own house. He makes strange signs on white paper and he gives orders. He demands obedience. White man does not work to provide himself with food. He cultivates certain plants which cannot be eaten; he keeps certain animals which also cannot be eaten and he hunts wild creatures which are neither dangerous nor edible. And yet he never goes hungry. Goods are sent to him in wooden boxes, in shining tins, in crates unloaded from ships, in containers dropped out of the sky. Things are sent to him which do not belong to this world, which could never be made in this world: matches, newspapers, hydrogen peroxide, corned beef, umbrellas and guns. His role is that of a receiver and he has the power of his endless supply of magical possessions. He is like a king surrounded by the rich fruits of his kingdom, like a victor with the spoils of a great battle, like a magician with magical weapons filled with energy. Always he is cloaked with that power which comes from his sense of right. He is not afraid of the priests and the rulers; he breaks the most sacred rules and taboos which govern a community. He insults the gods and he remains immune and invulnerable.

What then is the source of this power and this presumption? Where does it come from and in what is it contained? The white man has his

money and his god. The god is obviously stronger than other known gods, and is pleased with his white people. He might wear a hat, he might inhabit a factory in Germany, or a red land called Paradise. The missionaries instruct the people in the ways that they must approach this god and try to please him.

The people sing:
    Engiland side my words Papa God
    Engiland side Hallelujah Papa God
    Engiland side I come Papa God[2]

The people sing:
    Dark night time, night time Bethliem
    All sleep wake and get up
    Mother likes him child christ clean white baby.[3]

The people sing:
    God save our gracious King
    Long may he rain on us[4]

It is often believed that this god is the manufacturer of money. Certainly both he and it come from a distant and inaccessible land, whose exact whereabouts are known but not divulged by the white men. Certainly the one who is in possession of money is endowed with a spiritual strength which makes him superior to all those who have not got it. It is different from all other treasured articles: it is not a proof of achievement or of worth; it is a statement of possibility. The man who has money has future access to all that the heart might desire; he has the key to the infinite. In societies without a Western-style monetary system, the prestige and the status of an individual was something which had to be proved. The person who showed great courage, great virility or great wisdom won the respect of the whole community. The arrival of money makes all such criteria tumble, for the one who has it has the power, no matter what his capacities might be; the ones who have not got money are worthless, they are just 'rubbish men', all of them.

Before they were confronted by Western civilization, the people had myths and rituals which structured the rhythm of their daily lives and gave them a place within their own world. But the presence of the white men destroyed the traditional hierarchy and broke the continuity between the present and the past. A time of chaos was abruptly forced into being, a time in which there were no rules and no certainties. The old myths which told of how the world began but omitted to explain the origin of the whites can now no longer be trusted and new myths are needed. The old rituals, which ensured that the crops grew, that the men were successful in battle, that the women were not barren, are not able to provide supplies of tinned food, wads of paper money, guns; they do not protect the men from bullets or the children from the new diseases which strike them so suddenly. New rituals are needed. And the old gods, whoever they are, they need to become much stronger if they are to survive in the new pantheon which has presented itself, and maybe other gods should join them as well, the newly discovered powers of Jesus Christ, of Noah and Queen, and Jehovah.

No matter how strong their traditions or how firm their faith in their own intrinsic worth, the people are now exposed and vulnerable and they must enter a new age if they are to survive into the future. It is not possible simply to adapt to the white man; he is a cataclysmic event which threatens the spiritual survival of each group he encounters. Their

ABOVE
An unidentified colonial gentleman poses with a group of New Guinea islanders dressed in ceremonial costume. The place is a village called Motoa in the Mafulu Mountain region of Papua Central District (c.1925).

past is invalidated, or at least it is made into a limited aspect of a much larger past; their present is uncertain and chaotic and yet, somehow, with no clear guidelines to follow, there must be a change and a movement. Because the strength of the community as a whole has been undermined and scattered, each individual member finds himself defenceless and isolated. In order to rediscover some sense of personal dignity and right there must be a quest for salvation, an attempt to redefine those moral

qualities that distinguish the human world from the world of beasts.

When all the individual members of a community are estranged from their roles and obligations within the social structure, they need to find some other outlet for their hopes and aspirations. The community itself can no longer provide them with a sense of belonging, a sense of moral right, so they seek this reassurance elsewhere. Just beyond the borders of the visible world there are the gods, the spirits, the dead ancestors.

17

They stand in dense ranks, the accumulated energy of the history of a tribe or of a race. In such a time of crisis the people turn to them for help, knowing that these unseen presences must be listening and watching, eager to provide guidance. All that is needed is the language that will be understood by them, the correct rituals that will enable them to enter the world and assert their power among the living. And so it happens that in this state of tension and expectation, every aspect of life takes on a heightened meaning, a deeper and more profound symbolism. A dream becomes a vision; the rambling imaginings of a high fever become a revelation; a sudden sickness is the warning of impending disaster; a sudden return to health is the promise of eternal life. The world is filled with signs waiting for interpretation. Any man or woman who feels that he or she can act as an intermediary between heaven and earth needs only to speak and all will listen, command and all will obey.

Many of the texts in this anthology are based on the inspirations of solitary prophets who believed that in their dreams or in their waking visions they were being instructed by the gods, and that the gods had chosen them to try and help their people. In more stable times some of these new leaders would perhaps have been rejected by the society which welcomed them so enthusiastically, but now only those who are not afraid of the unknown, only those who feel that they can communicate with the unseen, can offer hope of salvation. The presence of white people forces a strangeness into the world; the prophets could face this strangeness and provide magical incantations and rituals which answered it in kind. When the prophet wept as he told of the armies of the dead who were waiting for their opportunity to join the living, the people wept and saw them too. When he trembled and shook, they did the same, and when he heard the heavy thudding of crates full of guns dropping to the ground, the earth shook with that sound. When he spoke a secret language, full of unknown words, no one failed to understand what was being said.

Many of the activities and statements coming from these prophets might seem strange and bizarre, but no matter what form this quest for salvation takes, it is always bound by a strong moral integrity. The people seek to find the 'right way' and each of the movements which has emerged during the last two centuries is the spontaneous product of a particular cultural background and its people's attempt to come to terms with the new age which has presented itself.

A number of communities were shaken with equal force during the beginning of the Christian era. Before it was adopted by the Roman Empire in the first decades of the fourth century, Christianity was a religion for those who felt themselves to be lost or oppressed. Christ's words spoke to those whose need for salvation was most urgent, who longed for the moment when God's power would be demonstrated on earth and the predictions of the Book of Revelation would be fulfilled, 'And I saw a new heaven and a new earth: for the first heaven and the

RIGHT
Portrait of the missionary and ethnologist P. Leo Bittremieux, who worked in the Catholic order of White Fathers in the western Congo and died in 1946. Work of the Woyo people from Moanda.

first earth were passed away; and there was no more sea . . . and there shall be no more death, neither sorrow nor crying, neither shall there be any more pain: for the former things are passed away.'[5] Within that apocalyptic time it must have seemed as if the world was about to shift on its axis, and everyone, anticipating the great upheavals that were soon to come, saw miracles and proofs of the existence of a living god all around them. Men spoke with angels and with devils; the blind were made to see and the dead to walk. Then, too, it was an age of prophecy, for the one who could see beyond the reality of the present moment was the one who could lead the faithful. People moved from elation to despair, from orgies of sensuality to asceticism and self-mortification. Some anticipated the Last Judgement in a frenzy of activity, others waited quietly for that moment when 'the stars of heaven and the constellations thereof shall not give their light: the sun shall be darkened in his going forth, and the moon shall not cause her light to shine'.[6] When the trumpet did not sound the signal for the lids of the graves to be flung open, and when the four horsemen of the Apocalypse did not appear on the horizon, even then there would be no indefinite loss of faith or hope. There had to be more questing through the darkness until finally the transition was accomplished. Hundreds of sects grew up, flowered briefly and were lost, but some survived as well, their ordered rules and principles born out of this time of chaos.

For the people who have to confront the colonizing process it is now a similar apocalyptic time. Often they too project their uncertainty and the inevitability of enormous changes on to the belief that the world itself must soon come to an end. Sometimes their anticipations might have been influenced by the teachings of the missionaries, but also such a response does seem to be the natural outcome of a huge psychic shock: the impact of Western civilization deprived them of the world as they had known it.

This anthology attempts to demonstrate the intrinsic logic of certain responses to the arrival and the continued presence of the white men. A great deal has been written about these responses, the leaders who instigated them, the factors which influenced a sudden burst of activity and those which caused everything to become quiet again. Here the people who were directly involved are allowed to speak for themselves. This is a collection of visions and revelations, of new mythologies and practical explanations, of instructions as to what should be done in the future and reminiscences about what happened in the recent past. The stories tell of how someone addressed a meeting, instructed a disciple or explained his impressions or his predicament to an anthropologist, a missionary or a policeman.

There are several inevitable constraints in making such a collection. None of the peoples represented had a written literature of their own, thus the only source has been the chance presence at a particular time and place of an interested outsider, able to listen, observe and write down all that he had learnt. Many of the movements were overtly anti-white in their sentiments or were at least seen as posing some kind of a threat to the white government; so, this observer must either have won the special confidence of a certain group, or the information has been extracted under pressure. It means that this anthology cannot be seen as a balanced study of responses to colonization, but is rather a selection of poetry and prose which is all related to aspects of one central theme. This applies equally to the pictures accompanying the texts. Only very rarely has it been possible to illustrate a particular story directly with a painting, carving or drawing made at the same time and in the same geographic region. Only very rarely does a photograph exist of the leader of a particular movement or of people performing one of the new ceremonies which the presence of the white men provoked. For the most part the images included here – missionaries, soldiers, books, umbrellas, crucifixes, aeroplanes and guns – are intended to provide visual embodiments of some of the themes and ideas occurring throughout the anthology.

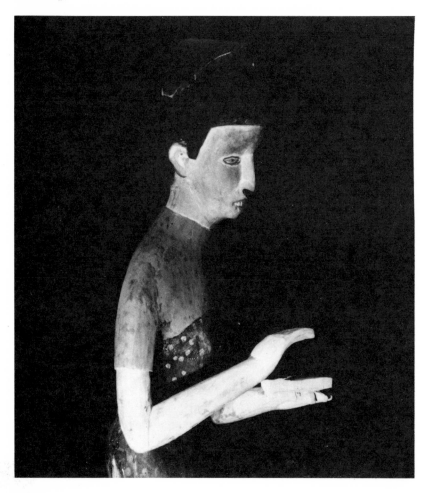

22

Always, however simple and apparently naïve their form of expression, these responses to the white men question the assumptions of power on which the white administration and political authority is based. Any such questioning is seen as a threat to the new establishment and a potential cause of anarchy which should be stamped out as quickly as possible. If a movement does survive, in spite of attempts to crush it, it must become increasingly subversive and also increasingly conscious of its underlying political ideology. Ironically, then, a number of the movements which are well represented here come from places which had little political or commercial importance and so were not so strictly watched over, or from peoples whose spirit was already so broken and whose numbers were so diminished, that they could pose no serious threat to the establishment, no matter what they did or said.

Some geographic areas have not been represented at all. This can be due to the fact that a race of people died out before any record was made of their manner of going. But also, it often happens that even when a detailed study has been made of a particular response to the white men, it is presented as a specialist work. Either the things that were said are not quoted in full, but only in brief excerpts used to illustrate a point, or they have been paraphrased into a smooth narrative which contains all

the relevant information, but destroys the identity of the one who was speaking.

Still there is much that can be said. There is the difference between reading about the Ghost Dance religion which spread among the Plains Indians between 1870 and 1890 and reading an account, even though derived from a longhand transcription translated into English, of how Short Bull addressed a gathering of the Sioux tribe, when he told them that the earth was going to shiver, a wind was going to blow and the dead would return to the living, and when he instructed them how they must confront the white men in battle: 'If the soldiers surround you four deep, then three of you on whom I have put holy shirts will sing a song which I have taught you. And when you sing this song around the soldiers, some of them will drop dead. Then the rest of them will start to run, but their horses will sink into the earth. . . . You must not be afraid of anything. The guns are the only things we are afraid of, but the guns belong to our father in heaven, and he will see that they do us no harm.'[7]

One can hear about how a conquered people often imitate the military disciplines, the style of dress and the words of command which they have seen and heard used by white men in an attempt to adopt the power of these unfamiliar rituals. But still it does not prepare one for the shock of the strange chanting incantation with which the Maori warriors involved in the Hau-hau movement of 1890 confronted the bullets of their enemies, confident that their words cloaked them in a magical invulnerability:

Kill, one, two three, attention!
North, north by east, nor nor east, northeasy, colony, attention!
Come to tea, all the men around the *niu* pole, attention!
Shem, rule the wind, too much wind, come to tea, attention![8]

The Australian Aborigines were among those who found it most difficult to adapt to the white strangers, so much so that they often died from a kind of quiet despair, unable to tolerate these people who did not believe that a child must first be conceived in a dream, who did not know the language of animals, who did not understand stones and trees and who could not identify a man by his footprint on the ground. In a recorded monologue made in 1950 in Arnhem Land, Australia, an Aboriginal woman explained with stark clarity the unease which all of her people must have experienced: 'That child had no sense, because they hadn't explained to him properly. He tried to cry, and urinated in fear when the white man touched his skin. He tried to run away, but those Aborigines standing nearby took hold of him. He tried to bite them; but at last they got a lot of those children and brought them to the dormitory. And they told them not to bite the white man's hand. They said to them, "You stay quiet with that white man, or he might shoot you with his gun!"'[9]

THE WHITE MEN ARRIVE

My children,
When at first I liked the whites
I gave them fruits,
I gave them fruits[1]
(Report of the Bureau of Ethnology 1892–3 by James Mooney)

I T IS AS IF CREATURES from outer space were to land in one of our cities. The news of their arrival travels at a desperate speed from place to place, from country to country. The simple facts of the situation become immediately confused with the private fears and imaginings of each individual who hears what has happened, and soon many wild and contradictory stories are in circulation.

There would be those who believe that the arrival of the white men must be a sign presaging the end of a troubled world, and they then realize that they have been expecting such an event for a long time. Others would perhaps trust that these are benevolent intruders who have been sent to help the human race and bring a new golden age into being. One person becomes hysterical and the mood infects a whole group, because this is a time for mass responses. Even if these strange creatures travel about very little and do no harm to their hosts, just the knowledge of their existence forces people to reassess completely their sense of their own place within the universe.

And something like this has been happening during the last two hundred years or so, to numerous, different, isolated groups of people, when the white men suddenly arrived in their country.

The Big Bird Comes

THE EASTERN HIGHLANDERS, Papua New Guinea

During the 1930s the drone of an aeroplane was heard for the first time in the Eastern Highlands of New Guinea. From that time until the early 1940s, rumours spread from village to village, telling that a 'big something' had arrived: strange creatures, not human beings but 'another kind', red-skinned, with only hands and face showing, who were carried in the belly of a great silver bird. It was not until the late 1940s and early 1950s that the people met white men for the first time.

When they first heard a plane the people thought its sound presaged some enormous disaster. And when they saw one, flying high overhead, they believed that the beings it carried must be their own ancestors returning in spirit form to the land of the living. But spirits were usually unpredictable, so they were disturbed and frightened. They were not sure whether the ancestors would be friendly or antagonistic. To meet

RIGHT
The Arrival of Captain Ambrose, the first District Commissioner, who came to the region in 1895, was commemorated in this detail from the carved wooden gates of the palace of the Ogogo of Ikerre Ekiti in southern Nigeria. It was carved by Olowe of Ise, Yoruba people.

26

this emergency, they performed a whole new set of rites to protect themselves from any possible danger.

From every village came news of the arrival of the Big Bird. Its strange noise made men and women afraid. They asked each other, 'What is that thing that cries? Could it be the sound of water? Could it be the sound of the earth breaking open? Or could it be just the cry of a cassowary bird?' All of us heard that noise.

Later the Big Bird flew overhead. Men and women saw it, that big something. 'If we look,' they said, 'we will die.' They threw themselves on the ground until it had passed over.

When the Big Bird had gone, they cooked pig fat and poured it on to croton leaves, breaking up the leaves to make them crinkly. They fastened these in their hair and tied them to their string bags, to propitiate this unknown thing, and to safeguard themselves against it.

Men and women talked among themselves. 'If we look at this thing, we will die, we will die! It comes and it goes: something, someone, must have made it.' And then we heard that white men, all covered up with clothing, had come to nearby places. Kamano men came and told us about the plane. They called it Mother Bird of the Sky. It carried men inside its belly, they said, and disgorged them when it reached the ground. Then some of us went to Kainantu. We saw it land, and saw men come out from it, and we knew we had been deceived – that it was not really a bird at all. But white men had come; and we thought to ourselves, 'This is something big, it is something we don't know about'.

The Wagons that Died

THE TATI BUSHMEN, Botswana, Southern Africa

Some thought that the wagons were huge animals which had crawled up out of the sea. They were impressed by the strength of these creatures, and horrified by the deep and footless tracks they made in the ground. And when the wagons were deserted and left silent and still, it seemed that they were sick and dying, for they never moved, neither did they eat any food.

This was in the 1830s when the Dutch Boers were moving inland and eastwards from the Cape Colony area, spurred on by their desire to establish new communities which would be beyond the reach and control of British colonial rule. The Tati Bushmen tell how they encountered one small and defeated group of trekkers, in the Lake Ngami region of Botswana. The account was recorded in the early twentieth century but the time it refers to must be the 1830s or 1840s.

The first time we saw wagons was when the Trek Boers went up to
Lake Ngami. We thought the wagons were big animals. There were
many oxen going before, and these big animals were going after, as
we thought. Some of the old Bushmen had seen such things before.
They looked like elephants, those wagons, but they were white.
We watched them a long time, and we saw that some of them stopped.
There was not much rain that year and the grass was not good. The
oxen were thin and then they died. Many died before they got to the
lake, and sometimes we had some of their flesh to eat.
At last one day we saw some of the Boers take all the cows out of the
wagon, and then they left it on the veld. We were afraid to go near it.
We thought they had left it to graze, but we saw that its feet did not
move. Some got near then, and we looked inside. There were lots of
things inside, but we Bushmen did not know their uses and so we
left them. We found some dry meat which we took.
Then we went on after the others and by and by we were near to the
wagons of the Boers, so they got their horses and galloped after us.
Three of us were caught. They tied up our hands and they told us to
take them to the water. I was young then. They tied us up at night,
but one of us got away in the darkness.
After a time all the cattle died of sickness and the Boers got sick and
died too. They left their wagons. At first when we saw them they
were living in their wagons. Many of the Boers were killed, many
died, and others went away. Some of the women were taken by the
Bechuana Bushmen but I don't know what they did with them.
We Bushmen never killed any of these people, but we took their
cattle and ate many of them. The wagons died on the veld, and some
of them were burnt. That is what I knew of the Boers. It is the end
of the tale.

La Pérouse at Lituya Bay

THE TLINGIT INDIANS, Alaska, North America

Lituya is a Tlingit word which means 'the lake within the point'. The Bay is a deep and narrow inlet almost cut off from the Pacific Ocean by the sand spits, ledges and bars which have formed at its mouth, and it can only be entered on a calm day at slack water. Once inside, the waters have an almost unnatural stillness about them and the area was a favourite haunt of the sea otter, and a favourite hunting ground of the Tlingit Indians.

In 1876 the French navigator La Pérouse discovered the opening to the Bay during his explorations of the Northwest coast. While he was still observing it from the outside he was abruptly swept in by the force of the tide. He remained in Lituya for 26 days and during this time he traded with the Indians and made a detailed account of the area and its inhabitants. His departure was even more dramatic than his arrival, for two of his small boats were sunk in the rough waters and the crew of 21 men was drowned.

In 1886 the story of this first encounter with the white men was told by a chieftain of the Tlingit and in this way the traditional recollections of the Indians and the written records of the Frenchman were able to verify each other. The version included here opens with another Tlingit account of the same event which was told in 1949. The narrator declared that these first white men seen by his people were the Russians, but all his information indicates that he must also be referring to the French expedition.

When they came to Lituya Bay, the people looked at the Russians through kelp, no, skunk cabbage leaves – like a spyglass, because they thought the Russians were land otters. Skunk cabbage leaves would protect them. The Indians thought the Russians were land otters disguised as people.

The Russians just came to the mouth of Lituya Bay in a big schooner - they don't come inside. They anchored out there. No one came ashore; no one went out to them. They were scared of one another.

One spring a large party of men from the big village at Kaxnuwu went to get copper from the people at Yakutat. Four canoes were lost at the entrance of Lituya Bay and the first chief of the party was drowned. While the survivors were still mourning, two ships rounded the bay. The Indians thought they were two great birds with white wings, perhaps Raven [2] himself. They fled to the woods. After a time they came back to the shore and looked through tubes of rolled-up skunk cabbage leaves, like telescopes, for if they looked directly at Raven they might turn to stone.

When the sails were made fast, they thought the birds folded their wings, and they imagined they saw a flock of crows fly up from the ships, so they ran back into the woods again.

One family of warriors dressed in armour and helmets, and took their
copper knives, bows and arrows, and launched a canoe. They were so
frightened when thunder and smoke came from the ship that their
canoe overturned and they scrambled ashore.

Then a nearly blind old man said his life was behind him, and he
would see if Raven really turned men to stone. He dressed in sea-
otter furs, and induced two of his slaves to paddle him to the ship.
When he got on board his eyesight was so poor that he mistook the
sailors for crows, and threw away the rice that was offered to him,
thinking it was worms. He traded his fur coat for a tin pan and
returned to shore laden with gifts of food.

The people were surprised to see the old man alive. They smelled him
to make sure that he had not been turned into a land-otter man, and
they refused to eat the food he had brought.

The old man finally decided that it must be ships and people he had
seen, so the Indians visited the ships and traded their furs. Then the
white men lost two boats at the mouth of the inlet and many were
drowned.

The Big-House-Ship

THE BOOANDIK ABORIGINES, South-east Australia

The Australian Aborigines of the south-east coastal region first encountered white men in the early 1820s, although they had probably seen
the distant lights of ships on the horizon before that time. This account
was given by an old woman of the Booandik tribe to a certain Mrs James
Smith, missionary and teacher. Mrs Smith and her husband worked
among these people for 35 years. She recorded her retirement and the
imminent extinction of what had once been a numerous and powerful
tribe in a little book published by the South Australian Government.
The greater part of this book is devoted to the 'Aborigines' capabilities
for evangelising and civilising', but the opening section includes a few
legends, customs and early reminiscences, such as this one.

The woman Pendowen said she saw the Big-house-ship and she was
afraid. She hid behind some bushes. She watched the *coomimor* which
is the name her tribe gave to the white men.

She said a large number of her people came like sheep to see the
Big-house-ship. She saw white women going away to the west. She
saw her own black people stealing the goods of these coomimor. She
did not know how many of the coomimor were there.

She said, 'My children and many more of the Booandik people went to
see those white men. I went too and I was very frightened. I saw
many things which I cannot name.'

She said, 'We were very hungry. We ate flour, that was very good, we
ate the floury root. We did not make bubble-bubble bread, we eat it

dry then. A child belonging to me died. Many of the children died. It must have been the flour that killed them. I did not bury my children. The white men went to the west.'

The Washani Religion

THE KLIKITAT INDIANS, Washington State, North America

In every tribe on the north-west coast area there were one or two dreamers – a man or a woman who suddenly became possessed with visionary powers and was able to communicate with the spirit world. There was a widespread belief that at a certain time the world was due to come to an end, and a dreamer could anticipate this disaster and help to avert it. He could read the meaning of fearful signs such as an earthquake or an eclipse of the moon, and he was also able to 'die' and enter the world of the dead to learn what was going to happen in the land of the living. It was said that the dead danced certain ritual dances before the Creator. The dreamer could learn these dances and the songs that accompanied them and could teach them to the people of his tribe. 'The dreamer proclaimed his dream and organized a dance. On the appointed day the people gathered out-of-doors in a circle around him. They wore no paint or special clothing, and used no drums, dance poles or other paraphernalia. They began to dance standing in a circle around the dreamer, the circle not revolving or the dancers changing their positions . . . . Occasionally someone had a prophetic dream during the ceremony, and at once uttered his prophecy to the people and took his place with the leader in the centre of the formation.'[3]

During the end of the eighteenth century and the beginning of the nineteenth, rumours about the white men – not actually seen until the

1840s – accelerated the need to communicate with the other world. There were countless strange signs to be interpreted and prophecies to be told. They said that a new race of men was coming, bearing gifts for the Indians. One woman saw a goose with two heads and four legs flying across the sky from the south-east; and this was realized to be the direction from which the whites were to be expected. A fall of white volcanic ash in the northern region west of the Rockies was interpreted as the proof that the world would soon end and the Indian nation would be destroyed. In quieter times the dream dances had lasted for perhaps a few days; now they became more compulsive and could go on for an indefinite period of time during which all normal life came to an abrupt halt, 'All spring, all summer and on into the fall they danced. All other activities were suspended, no one hunted or fished or gathered berries. They simply danced all day and every day, standing in one spot. When winter came there was no food in store, and many people starved.'[4]

A similar story is told here. A woman of the Klikitat tribe was asked to give an account of the origin of the Washani religion. She was interviewed in 1934, and the period she refers back to was sometime before 1830. The word *washani* means dancers, and this religion was one of the first of the many waves of prophecy and dancing which swept through American Indian tribes of the Plains and the west coast when they were confronted by the white men.

In the old days before the whites came, the Indians had many trances,
  That is how the Washani religion got started. Long before even my
  grandmother's time, a woman in Columbia had things revealed to
  her. She died and came back to life and told all she had seen.
She said a people with white hair and skin and eyes were coming. She
  said they had different materials to work with, different clothing,
  different food that they would give to the Indians.
Then they all got excited like the Seventh Day Adventists. They sang
  and danced all day and all night. They went crazy. They burnt all
  their things, or threw them all in the river. They destroyed
  everything because the whites were coming to give them everything.
That summer they didn't store up any food. Only a few of the wise
  ones saved everything they'd got. They had a bad winter that year.
  Many began to starve and the whites did not come. The wise ones
  tried to keep the others fed.
In the spring they found many who had crawled off, trying to get
  food, and had died of weakness.

Something Strange is Creeping Across the Waters

THE KUANYAMA AMBO, Namibia and Angola, Africa

The prophet of King Haimbili told how an elephant had broken into the royal garden, a sign that the king was doomed to die soon.

LEFT
A wooden statue of a white man and his dog. The figure is festooned with a variety of magical emblems, and was probably used in a healing cult. It was made by the Kongo people around the turn of the century.

The elephant brings evil,
When it comes into the king's garden.
So it has happened, why is it so?
In Ondonga they must let the white men pass.
The white men will come here also, to this garden.[5]

This took place shortly after 1851, the date when white missionaries arrived in Ondonga, in the southern part of the Ambo region. These, then, were the first intimations of the imminent collapse of a powerful African kingdom.

Haimbili was revered as the greatest of the known Ambo kings; he was also the last of them to be given all the attributes of a semi-divine being. All land, cattle and subjects belonged to him. He was above any laws and he controlled the vagaries of the weather. His kingdom was ruled according to a feudal system of nobles and serfs, and when his reign was considered to have come to its end, he was ritually murdered by his servants to ensure that he would not interfere with the powers of his successor.

Haimbili died in 1861, and from this time onwards the Ambo kings became less and less powerful both in spiritual and in temporal matters. The last king in the line was Mandume who was killed in 1917. After that the Ambo were ruled by headmen and subheadmen who were in their turn answerable to white government officials.

The poem included here is made up of two prophecies which follow on from each other both in time and in what they are responding to. The first two sections date from the 1870s when the white missionaries were moving northwards into the Kuanyama region and the last section probably dates from the 1890s. Here the prophet Muselanga laments not only the fact that the white men have come to his country, but also the fact that his king Oejulu has befriended them.

Something strange is creeping over the waters;
Foreigners creep into the country.
It was far, it comes near, it is here.
People start to walk.
Perhaps an *omuhama* tree will fall across their path.
The strange people come from a distant country,
They come with different words.
When they are talking they should be listened to.

I walked and walked through the country
And I saw the kraals of the nobles.
I walked a second time through the country
I did not see the kraals of the nobles
But white men's houses I have seen.

Oejulu! I do not see the kraal of the King.

I do not see the kraals of the nobles.

Only the kraal of the woman Naminda I see.

White men's houses I see in what were the fields of Haindongo.

Houses I see like white millet meal.

The world will end, it will end completely.

The King will die, he will go underground to the palace of the frog.

I will go away from here, I will go underground into the hole of the bees.

I will go in a clothing of earth

For I have cursed the King.

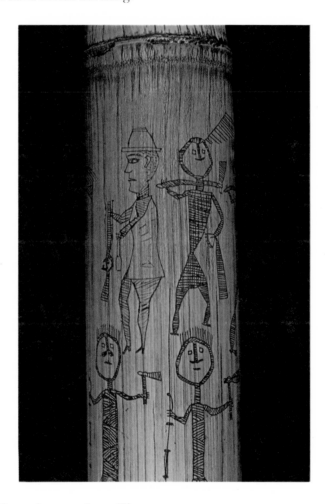

The Man who saw them First

THE EASTERN HIGHLANDERS, Papua New Guinea

The Big Bird had been heard in the sky, and some people had seen it. Some had even seen the men it contained. But the fact remained that 'something big' had happened. Rumours continued to circulate from one district to another, and the people were still fearful of what might happen. They felt the arrival of the strangers might be dangerous, and so would touching anything that belonged to them. Something would have to be done to avert the danger. They took special leaves – usually eaten as a relish with pig meat – chewed them, and spat them over the food, dividing the meat among them. Eating such leaves would protect them. Later, some cloth was sent down to them by the Kamano people. This was something they had not seen before, and feared; they rubbed it with special leaves, and then swallowed them. When they met men who had actually seen the strangers, they rubbed the men's eyes with these leaves, and ate them. The leaves, they believed, had absorbed some of the new power. Swallowing the leaves brought them into intimate contact with it, neutralizing any harmful effects it might have.

Although the people were afraid, they were also curious. Some of them organized a courtship excursion to a place in Kamano country, hoping their dancing and feasting might attract the strangers. But the strangers did not arrive.

White men came to Kainantu. 'Why do they come there?' people ask. Stories are passed on to the southern districts about these white people. 'His name is white man,' they say, 'but he is something big, not really a man but of another kind'. He came, this man, and we looked at him. His skin was red, and we saw only his face and hands; the rest of his body was all hidden, all covered with clothes.

Men in the southern part of the country asked, 'Why did they come?' They were all afraid in their bellies; some looked at the white men, but feared them. They all talked in this way. So they took special leaves, and gave them to the Kamano people to protect themselves. And they themselves chewed such leaves and spat out the juice over their meat.

Some of the people went north to a place named Tirokai, far from their own villages. There they built a mountain house and held courtship dances. They said, 'The white men will come to see us doing this'. When the house was finished, they danced. They danced day and night. They killed pigs and spat the juices of special leaves on to the meat.

Later some cloth came down to the southern people. They all looked at it. They had seen nothing like it before. And a man told them, 'Get *migufa* leaves, rub them on the cloth, then eat the leaves'. He added, 'You might die seeing new things, if you don't do this'.

Men from Fomu village had seen the white men first. The others asked them, 'Is it true you looked at the white men?' They replied, 'Yes, we have looked at them'. They rubbed leaves on their eyes, and ate them. But the white men did not come to Tirokai, where the mountain house was built. We thought they would have come but they didn't – only those with skin like us were there.

ABOVE
Two men fight with each other while a third stands by, apparently ignoring them, in this curious, theatrical scene on a bamboo pole from New Caledonia.

How Snakes Crawl Inside the Women

THE EASTERN HIGHLANDERS, Papua New Guinea

Distorted rumours spread fan-wise to the southern districts from
Kainantu, where a European patrol post had been established in the
early 1940s. It was said that snakes, sent by the Europeans, would come
to the villages, enter pregnant women and kill their unborn children. To
prevent this, their husbands made skin aprons, which they hung round
their necks to hide their distended bellies and so deceive the snakes. To
make doubly sure, they fastened beaten bark round their genitalia.
In spite of this, some women were so frightened that they aborted
themselves. Abortion had not been known in this area before this
happened.

They say that, now white men have come, all pregnant women will
   die. Their husbands killed pigs, cutting off the breast skin and
   hanging it from the necks of their pregnant wives to hide their
   dilated bellies.
'Why does this happen?' they asked. 'Now a snake comes crawling,
   entering the vulvas of women.' They make beaten bark cloth as loin
   coverings, fastening it around them to prevent the snake from
   entering them. Some women are so afraid, that they kill the children
   in their bellies; they kill and bury them so that no snake will crawl
   inside them.
Because of the white men at Kainantu, a special spirit of the dead
   comes, and with him a long snake and a little one: they come
   crawling, looking for women to enter. Rumours said this would
   happen.
The men built a large house and latrine for the women. They also
   built a stockade around the house. They stored up firewood, made
   bark cloth, and put them in the house, along with their sacred
   objects. They went to the gardens, dug sweet potatoes and yams, cut
   bananas, and filled bamboo containers with water. All these things
   they put in the house, they filled it up.
Then the women and the children and men all went into that house,
   and remained there. The women fastened bark cloth tightly around
   their loins. The special flowers they had picked they now chewed,
   and sprayed the blue juice over the pregnant women. While the
   women slept separately, the men watched over them until the
   daylight came. They killed pigs; they took croton leaves and
   sprinkled blood over the meat, and on the door posts of the house:
   and they rubbed blood over the pregnant women. They killed pigs,
   and gave meat to the women. They slept.
Ten days passed by. The firewood was finished, the food was
   finished. 'We have been deceived,' they said. And they left the house.
   They killed pigs and sprinkled blood about the house and over the
   women. They removed the bark coverings from the women and

threw them away. 'The Kamano men have deceived us,' they said. 'The Kamano men said the spirit of the dead would come, and the little snakes would come . . . they have deceived us.' It was all because the white men came, and we looked at you. All of you deceived us. We did this because of you.

The Coming of the Wasichu

THE LAKOTA SIOUX INDIANS, The Plains, North America

Black Elk was a Sioux Indian, a member of the Lakota tribe. He was born in the 'Moon of the Popping Trees' which is December, in the 'Year When the Fox Crow Indians were Killed' which was the year of 1863. At the age of nine he became suddenly ill and lay in a coma for many days. During this time he had a vision which changed the entire course of his life. He was led to a place 'beyond the flaming rainbow', and brought before the ancestors. They told him that he had been chosen to help the Indian people in their time of trouble and taught him magical songs and the use of certain healing herbs. They also gave him gifts and showed him great things. When Black Elk recovered he was afraid of everything and silent; and his family thought that he had been turned crazy by the sickness. It was not until he was in his late teens that he was finally persuaded to tell what he had seen and heard. Then his people made preparations for a great feast. They learned the songs he told them and they painted magical signs on the horses and made magical masks and costumes. When everything was ready Black Elk's vision of the ancestors was re-enacted on earth. From this time he was again able to communicate with his fellows and he became a leading prophet and medicine-man not only for his own tribe but for many groups of Plains Indians.

Black Elk was born in that crucial period of American history when the Plains Indians had to make a completely new life for themselves or die out. Their lives were centred on the great wandering herds of buffalo and between the 1870s and the early 1880s these creatures were being speedily and wantonly exterminated by the white men. Black Elk's self-appointed task was to try and provide his people with some sort of spiritual framework which would give them the strength and the determination to survive.

In 1930 a white American by the name of John Neihardt went to meet Black Elk. By this time he was a blind old man, living on a reservation. Though haunted by his memories and his sense of failure, he was still able to cure the sick and to 'read the darkness in men's eyes'. He decided that the story of his life must be written down before his death, and so, with the help of his son as a translator, he recounted his memories to John Neihardt. This excerpt from his book *Black Elk Speaks* goes back to his early childhood. He tells of the arrival of the Wasichu, as the white men were called, and of an event which he remembers only as 'some

fearful thing in a fog'. In this 'Battle of the Hundred Slain' 81 American soldiers were killed by the Lakota Indians at a place called Peno Creek on 21 December 1866.

I had never seen a Wasichu then, and did not know what one looked like; but everyone was saying that the Wasichus were coming and that they were going to take our country and rub us out and that we should all have to die fighting. It was the Wasichus who got rubbed out in that Battle of the Hundred Slain, and all the people were talking about it for a long while. But a hundred Wasichus was not much if there were others and others without number where those came from.

I remember once I asked my grandfather about this. I said: 'When the scouts come back from seeing the prairie full of bison somewhere, the people say the Wasichus are coming; and when strange men are coming to kill us all, they say the Wasichus are coming. What does it mean?' And he said, 'That they are many'.

BELOW
The Battle of One Hundred Slain as it was drawn by the Dakota Indian Standing Bear to illustrate Black Elk's narrative of his life.

44

When I was older I learned what the fighting was about that winter
and the next summer. Up on the Madison Fork the Wasichus had
found much of that yellow metal that they worship and that makes
them crazy, and they wanted to have a road up through our country
to the place where the yellow metal was; but my people did not want
the road. It would scare the bison and make them go away, and also
it would let the other Wasichus come in like a river. They told us
that they wanted only to use a little land, as much as a wagon would
take between the wheels; but our people knew better. And when you
look about you now, you can see what it was they wanted.

Once we were happy in our own country and we were seldom hungry,
but then the two-leggeds and the four-leggeds lived together like
relatives, and there was plenty for them and for us. But the
Wasichus came, and they have made little islands for us, and other
little islands for the four-leggeds, and always these islands are
becoming smaller, for around them surges the gnawing flood of the
Wasichu; and it is dirty with lies and greed.

A long time ago my father told me what his father told him, that there
was once a Lakota holy man, called Drinks Water, who dreamed
what was to be; and this was long before the coming of the
Wasichus. He dreamed that the four-leggeds were going back into
the earth, and that a strange race had woven a spider's web all
around the Lakotas. And he said, 'When this happens, you shall live
in square grey houses, in a barren land, and beside those square
grey houses you shall starve'.

The Landing of Alvaro de Mendana

THE SANTA ISABEL ISLANDERS, *Solomon Islands*

The Spanish explorer and navigator Alvaro de Mendana discovered the
Solomon Islands in 1567. He landed at first on an island which he named
Santa Isabel. There in the Bay of Gehe he organized his men into building
a brig which they could use for making a survey of the other islands.

The descendants of the people who first saw, and were seen by
Mendana, are now almost extinct. However, when this account was
collected in 1947 there were still a few men who claimed to be related to
the original Gehe people. One man even said that he was the great-great-
great-great-great grandson of the chief Belenbangara who came down to
the beach to see the first white men and receive gifts from them.

The people already had a religious tradition about a distant land of the
dead inhabited by ghosts. The white men were quickly recognized as
ghosts, but ghosts coming from an unknown family group who were
therefore unapproachable and feared. The people had always blamed the
ghosts for many illnesses, and once the unfamiliar diseases of the white
men had taken effect, this old belief must have taken on an increased
significance. The ships themselves took on a magical power of their own,

so that their arrival was dreaded. Even today the people call the white man's speech 'ship talk', and the place where he comes from, be it Australia or a nearby plantation, is known as the 'place of the ship'.

As soon as they saw the white men come ashore, they thought that
  they must be ghosts, and they ran to the bush. The white men
  shouted after them, but, in their terror, they ran to the bush.
After this, great thunder burst above their heads, which came from
  the firing of the muskets.
For days they stealthily came to find out what manner of beings the
  white men were, and also to find out whether they were real men, or
  ghosts.
For days they could not make contact with the white men, but, little
  by little they came nearer, as the white men showed signs of being
  friendly.
Then a man gave himself up. He simply walked over to the white men
  and they received him with kindness. Not only were they friendly
  but they gave him some of their goods, they gave him mirrors and
  beads and pieces of cloth.
Finally Belenbangara made his appearance, and he let it be known by
  signs that he was the chief of the people. The white men gave him
  presents and he in turn gave them food.
The people watched how the white men built a great canoe. They
  were very much surprised at the speed of the great work.
The white men stayed on the island for at least ten moons. The people
  called their ship the *nguanguao*, and they said that it was manned by
  ghosts and it carried diseases. They said that the white men were also
  ghosts.
Later whenever the people saw a ship approaching they told their
  women and children to hide, and the men prayed to the spirits,
  asking them to remove the nguanguao ship, this disease carrier.

Ongka's Narrative

THE MOUNT HAGEN HIGHLANDERS, Papua New Guinea

In 1933 two explorers in search of gold, Michael and Dan Leahy, and an Australian government officer called J L Taylor came by air and foot patrol to Mount Hagen, an area which had scarcely been penetrated by Europeans before then. The Hageners were a wealth-orientated people. Until this time the pearl and cowrie shells which they valued so highly came to their remote region with great difficulty, travelling from hand to hand along the traditional trade routes from the coast. When they first encountered the 'red men' their initial shock was soon replaced by delight, for now they were suddenly able to obtain precious supplies of shells as well as steel tools to replace their own finely polished stone axes and wooden spades.

Ongka, who is today a leader of one of the Hagen tribes and renowned for his wealth and his skill as a speech maker, was at that time a young man. He tells of how his people received the strangers, and of his disappointment when his father exchanged a pig for a cowrie shell when he could just as well have become the recipient of a steel axe.

All three explorers settled permanently in the Highlands, working as plantation owners and cattle ranchers. Jim Taylor, whose name is legendary throughout the area, became a naturalized citizen of Papua New Guinea when the country gained its independence in 1975.

When the first planes of the white men came, I was down by a stream.
There were several of us, old men and young boys, all working at

47

shaping stone axes. I thought I heard the voice of one of those marsupials that growl as they go along and have tails like lizard tails. We chased the noise through the undergrowth; it kept moving in front of us and we couldn't catch it. Then we looked up and saw it was in the sky and we said, 'It's a kind of witchcraft come to strike us and eat us up!' We argued about it: was it really witchcraft, or was it a big hornbill bird or an eagle? Some said it was a thunderclap gone mad and come down from the sky. Then it went away and we said we would find out about it later.

We did not know it had landed at Hagen. There were so many wars between groups all the way from us to Hagen, how could we go to see? Eventually someone did go all the way and returned to tell us that a foreign man with plenty of wealth in pearl shells had set up a house of bark cloth at Kelua near to Ogelbeng. He had come down in the flying thing and was living there. Later we saw Jim Taylor himself, he came through and called out for supplies for his many carriers. People took sugar-cane, sweet potatoes, bananas and pigs to him. He would draw out of his long trouser pockets a big mottled cowrie shell of the kind we valued, and show it to them, and they said, 'Oh! He has a big cowrie, and he's drawn it out of his own behind!' That was how we got to know the white man.

In the past we used long wooden sticks for a spade. We dug ditches, the men holding the spades, the women getting down into the trench and pulling up the lumps of earth with their hands. Then Taylor brought us real spades, knives and axes, and cowrie shells as well. After him came Michael and Dan Leahy who lived at Kuta, sluicing the river for gold, and paying people with shells too. One day two men from that area brought some of the large new cowrie shells down to Mbukl. One of them had a name Kuta Wak. I was away when my father met the men, and offered them a big pig in return for this special shell with the name. I heard about the visit of these strangers on my way back home, and I later asked my father why he had given away his finest pig to get the shell Kuta Wak. He said, 'Don't say anything about it! Pigs are things that we eat up and leave their bones in the cult houses dedicated to the spirits. It doesn't matter!' But I was thinking of how one of the new steel axes could slice right through a tree, and I was cross and I said, 'Why did you get a worthless shell? With a steel axe think of the work we could do.' Then my father told me to be quiet, for he had bought the cowrie in order to obtain a wife for me. I said, 'I don't want a wife, I want a steel axe', and we had a big row about it. 'You have no wife,' he said. 'Don't you know I want to get one for you? The white men are here and they'll be bringing plenty more axes for you, now this special shell is for your bride.' 'I don't want a bride, I want an axe,' I repeated. However, the men led the pig away, and I said no more about it, and so my father got me a wife.

WHITE MAN'S SECRETS

A white man looks at a piece of paper and laughs.[1]
(The Religious System of the Amazulu by H. Callaway)

T HE WHITE MEN HAVE POWER. It is different from the power possessed by warriors or chieftains which has been fought for and has to be maintained. The white men are passive and their power sits upon them like an invisible cloak. They apparently do not need to participate in the usual struggle for survival, and even when they are in a strange land with no family and no territory they immediately assume a position of absolute authority. It is as if they are perpetually watched over by supernatural agencies, loved and favoured by the most mighty gods.

The white men bring with them weapons that can kill in a way that killing has never been known; they bring food that does not need to be hunted or grown and quantities of other strange goods which no human could ever make. Shining boxes drop out of the sky; wooden containers are rowed ashore from ships that keep their distance; roads and railways are constructed to enable lorries, wagons and trains to bring in their enormous loads. The white men need only sit and wait and these things – the cargo[2] – comes to them. Without question they claim it all as their own.

The possession of quantities of food, or of rare and valuable commodities, is always recognized as an overt demonstration of wealth and power. The white men have matches, leather shoes, hydrogen peroxide, razor blades and tinned food; they have radios, motor bikes and rifles. Their cargo makes them the natural lords of all they survey; no one can compete with them or try to challenge their status. And yet, what have they done to obtain it? They have not hunted or prepared the soil or worked in any way. They have simply waited, written signs on pieces of paper, given orders and waited some more. Miraculously all that they desire appears before them.

The white men say that they come from a distant land where the cargo is made. This land often seems indistinguishable from the place inhabited by their god. Heaven lies beyond a white mist, its other name is 'Engiland'. Paradise is a red land which floats 30 miles above the town of Sydney in Australia. The god of the white men emerges as a bowler-hatted, black-waistcoated gentleman who manages an enormous factory in Germany where rice-in-bags and razor blades are produced and reproduced in ceaseless abundance. The people are often eager to please this high being. They give up their old customs, rituals and beliefs; they sing the new songs and build the new buildings; and wait for the moment when their period of initiation is over and they are rewarded with as much power and as many possessions as the white men now have.

RIGHT
These two formally dressed gentlemen with umbrellas, depicted on a bamboo pole from New Caledonia, are probably French officials.

In the world as the people knew it before, the aid of the gods was evoked for every aspect of life. If it happened that the crops failed, the women were barren, the enemies victorious or game scarce, it meant that the gods were angry, and their forgiveness and the renewal of their favour must be granted before the pattern of life could be re-established. It was obvious that the white men knew exactly what prayers and what rituals were necessary in order to please their god. And yet, when the people followed the instructions that they were given in order to have a share of this approval, they remained unregarded and unrewarded. No cargo dropped out of the sky into their gardens; no wooden crates filled with guns and knives were delivered to them. Instead they found themselves with less power than they had had before.

If the new god rejects the people it must be because the white men are not instructing them correctly. It must be that the white men have a secret that they do not wish to share. They know something vital about the true nature of their god, his origin, the place that he inhabits and the way that he wants to be worshipped. They are deceiving the people because in their greed they wish to keep everything – all the power and all the possessions – to themselves.

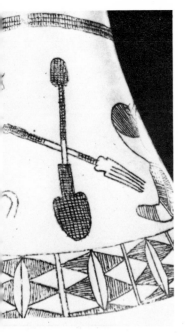

The people must try to find out the truth that lies behind all these deceptions, they must attempt to find this god of the white men on their own and speak with him directly. They have no past experience to reassure them and their priests and wise men are unable to provide any clear leadership and so they are forced to confront what is to them an absurd and unjust situation with only the inspiration of the present moment to guide them. Those who are able to transcend the boundaries of the perceived world can perhaps help the others. But the prophet, the visionary, or the man or woman who falls shaking into a trance is able to provide some guidance to the others. One man realizes that the white men have torn out the first page of the Bible, the page which explains how Jehovah and Jesus sailed out across the sea from the Island of Fiji. A South American Indian called Bichiwung goes to England and there he meets God who gives him the Indian Bible contained in a bottle. It is discovered that cargo is sent regularly to the people, but the white men have been intercepting it and that is why they spend so much of their time watching the horizon through their telescopes. Whole villages might destroy all their possessions and then sit, colonial-style, around white-clothed tables decorated with vases of flowers, waiting in silence for the boxes to arrive. Groups of men and women are possessed by variations of the 'head-he-go-round'[3] madness during which they might learn to write English so that they too can send orders and instructions to the land of infinite wealth. The people sing new songs and build new ceremonial houses, and try in many many ways to make it possible for the god of the white men to reward them with the material proof of his love.

Efforts are inevitably made to check such movements. Some are brought to an abrupt end and are soon forgotten, or they might go underground to re-emerge in a new mythology of lost wealth and invincible heroes. It can also be that the basically nationalistic and anti-white spirit which underlies all such movements and uprisings is unified into a new religious organization or a practical political force. Always, the white men's protestations and attempts to maintain control serve as the proof that they do have secrets which they want to keep hidden.

LEFT
A fashionable nineteenth-century gentleman dressed in a fitted jacket and with his hair meticulously groomed. This little terracotta figurine comes from the lower Congo regions of Africa.

RIGHT
On the henta boards from the Nicobar Islands the power of the white man is epitomized in the figure of the god Deuse. Here he bears a marked resemblance to a ship's captain, standing amongst a curious array of furniture and trade goods.

Mambu Goes to Australia

THE TANGU, North-east Papua New Guinea

Between the years 1937 and 1938 Mambu was a prophet for the Tangu people of Papua New Guinea. Not much is known about his life: he was baptized a Roman Catholic by the Australian Mission, he went to the island of Rabaul as a migrant worker, and when he returned in 1937 he had a revelation about what the white men were really doing. His teachings were not well received by his own coastal people, but they were by the inland Tangu people among whom he created a considerable disturbance. Mambu became the black king of the area. He told the people that they must not pay taxes to the white men, must not work for them and instructed them not to go into the mission churches. He explained that for a long time the ancestors had been working in a factory on the island of Manam where they manufactured cargo. They sent this cargo regularly over to New Guinea, but the white men had control over the ports and they kept intercepting it and keeping it for themselves. This injustice would not go on for ever: soon the ancestors would load up big ships, a harbour would appear just near Mambu's house, and the cargo would be brought ashore. There would follow a great holocaust in which the white men would all be killed along with any islanders who had persisted in being obedient to them.

Mambu established new ritual practices which used the mission teachings as their inspiration. Little churches were erected in several villages with a long pole sticking out above the circular roof and a cross and a red flag fixed to the pole. The people were told to bury their native clothes and to dress in European costume. That way when the ancestors arrived they would be pleased and would say, 'Ha! Our children are doing well!'

Mambu was arrested and imprisoned in 1938 and nothing more was heard of him, but his teachings survived and the myths grew and became the vehicles for several outbreaks of cargo activity in the north-eastern part of Papua New Guinea.

The anthropologist who recorded this version of the story in 1952 explains how the Mambu myth is told in a very different manner to the old island myths, such as the man who went to the moon on a betel nut or the two sisters who lived with an enormous penis, because Mambu's gift of cargo, his visit to Australia and his revelations about the ancestors, are historic events from the recent past coincident with the arrival of the missionaries, the great sickness and the Japanese invasion. And when the people tell this story they do so with great solemnity because it is the myth which is most relevant to their present situation.

Mambu was a native of the Bogia region in Tangu. He worked for a while in Rabaul and then stowed away on a steamer bound for Australia. Before long Mambu was discovered and brought before the captain.

The captain was very angry. He was going to have Mambu thrown overboard, because he knew that he might find the secret of the white men if he got to Australia. But Mambu's former master was on the same ship, and he intervened and saved him from the captain's anger.

The master was an Australian and he saw Mambu safely to an Australian port.

Once he had got to Australia, Mambu was clothed and fed. His master showed him the sights and gave him rice, spare clothing, beads, knives, canned goods, razor blades, and many other good things.

All this cargo was packed into cases and sent to the quayside for loading. The master's sister wrote a letter and stuck it into Mambu's hair. She told him to go down to the quay where he would find all his cargo marked with a certain sign. He was to collect his cargo and board a ship which was lying at the wharf, and then return to New Guinea. She said that if there was any trouble or if anyone questioned him, Mambu only had to show his letter and everything would be alright.

Mambu boarded his ship. The captain tried several times to throw him overboard, but he survived and eventually he reached Bogia.

If he had not had that letter he would have been killed.

When he was home again, Mambu said that he knew the secret of the white men. He said that the white men were jealous and that was why they prevented the people of New Guinea from sharing the secret too. Mambu said that the people of New Guinea should not submit to this, they must be strong and throw the white men out of New Guinea and into the sea. In order to make themselves strong they needed money.

So it was that Mambu travelled around the countryside collecting shillings and pennies. When a missionary reported him for doing this, he was sent to jail. This was because he was dangerous to the

LEFT
A group of men from the island of Malekula posing rather self-consciously with guns and a random collection of western clothing and goods. The photograph was taken by Bernard Deacon, who went to Malekula in 1926, and died there in the following year.

white men and might destroy their power and their authority.

When the policemen came to arrest him, Mambu said, 'You can hit me – never mind! You can maltreat me – never mind! Later you will understand.'

The policemen were very impressed, but they took him to prison just the same.

That night when Mambu was supposed to be behind bars in prison, Mambu was seen in a nearby village, chewing areca nut. He had escaped out of his chains.

The policemen knew about this but they were afraid to report it, because then they might be punished for neglecting their duties.

But Mambu could not escape altogether, and the administration caught him and took him away to the island of Madang in chains.

Before he left New Guinea he prophesized the war that was to come.

There was another thing that Mambu did. One of the men here went to test him to see if he was genuine. And Mambu took money out of thin air for him, and gave it to the man and the man went to the trade store and bought an axe and some beads with the money. Mambu had said to him, 'You do not understand. You are like a child who has to learn much. You do not understand the things that I know.' Mambu could get hold of money whenever he wanted to.

The Day of the Crocodiles

THE FANG, Gabon, West-Central Africa

In common with several other African Bantu tribes, the Fang have a tradition which tells of how they migrated southwards many generations ago. In their songs they still refer to the race of people who were their rulers and oppressors, calling them the Bethonas. As with 'All People Come from the Same Place' on page 112, this legend has been modernized so that it now explains the reason why the black and the white races became separated and also the means whereby the white men gained access to the infinite riches which are to be found in a land across the waters.

This story was written down, in a much lengthier version, by a missionary called P H Trilles who worked in the French Congo around the turn of the century. I have simplified his rather ornate prose in the process of translating it from the French.

There were white men and there were black men. White served black and black served white. It did not matter. They were equal.

One day there was a big quarrel between them. Neither side wanted to give in. Only Nzame could decide who was in the right. He ruled over all men, the white and the black.

Nzame lived alone in the centre of the black man's land. To reach him it was necessary to cross over a great forest. His hut was large, tall as

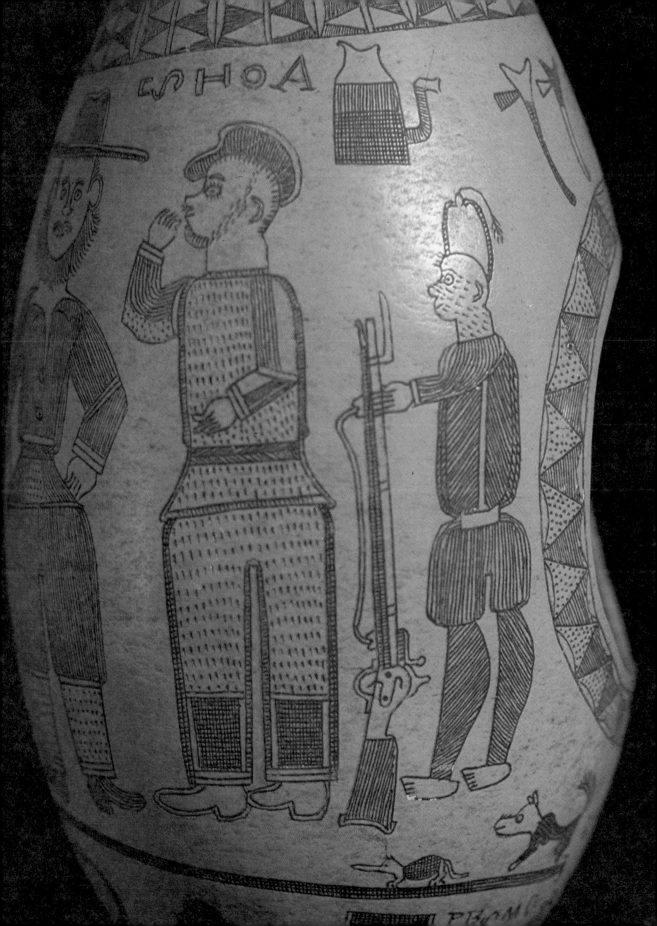

a tree, and the walls were made of woven bamboo. He was sitting next to a fire on a gnarled tree trunk. On his head was a big red cap. Round his neck hung necklaces of pearls and animal teeth. He wore a loin cloth with a red border.

Nzame said, 'I can never decide who is in the right. It would be better to separate you, and give you each your own land and your own ruler. This world is divided into two halves; in one half can be found many beautiful things, guns, necklaces, bracelets, everything. In the other half there is almost nothing. Now tell me, you black men, which half do you choose?'

And because both the black men and the white men wanted to have the rich land, Nzame decided to set them three tests. The whites won the first two tests. This is what happened with the final test.

Nzame led them to a big deep river. The current was fast, so fast that it was fearful to see. All along the bank lay crocodiles with their mouths wide open.

'You must cross this river,' said Nzame. 'Use this tree to make a bridge.' So they cut down the tree, and its trunk was long and straight and very narrow. When it fell across the river it did not quite touch the bank on the other side, instead it hung there, a short distance from firm ground, trembling above the water. The tree trunk trembled along its whole length.

'Now listen,' said Nzame, 'tonight it is too late. Tomorrow is the time for this last test.'

Quickly the white men built themselves huts. Then they built a small fire and went to sleep. Quickly the black men built a big fire, and they began to dance around it. They found palm wine to drink, and they danced the *Bekukua* dance all through the night.

The next morning Nzame said, 'On the other side of this river lies the rich land. To reach it you must cross over the bridge.'

A black man went first. He set his foot upon the bridge and, vlou! he fell, and, clic clac! a crocodile ate him. A second went and, vlou! he fell into the water and clic clac! A third, clic clac! A fourth, clic clac! They all fell in.

> Clic clac clic clac
> The day of the crocodiles.
> Clic clac the day of the black men
> Teeth below, misery above
> Clic clac, worship the crocodile
> Clic clac my heart is heavy
> Eyes, mouth and sharp white teeth.

And the black men sat by the bank of the river and looked across at the rich land that they would never know.

Then it was the turn of the white men. They did not fall.

Let us go to the dance
Those men have crossed over
They are on the other side
Here the fire is hot and red
They laughed at us
Let us go to the dance.

When the last white man was over the bridge the water of the river rose up, and the river got wider and wider. And as the white men got smaller and smaller, the river went on getting wider.
Now it takes many days travelling to get to the rich land. It is too far away now.

Paliau and Jesus

THE MANUS ISLANDERS, Admiralty Islands, Papua New Guinea

In the past all the white men have lied to us. All the missionaries have lied to us. They brought the name of Jesus and of his church. They told of his coming to earth and of his work and of his death for our redemption. But the true talk of Jesus, this they didn't tell us. But now I have found this. I, myself, have found it.'[4]

In 1884 the Admiralty Islands were declared a German protectorate; in 1914 the Australians took over. In 1942 they were occupied by the Japanese who were in turn driven out by the Americans in 1944, and in that same year the Islands were handed back to the Australians. It was during the American offensive that Paliau received the vision and the divine instruction that was to inspire him to become a leader of the people of Manus Island.

At the outbreak of the Second World War he had left his own small island of Baluan and was serving as a policeman in the town of Rabaul in Papua New Guinea. During the extensive bomb attacks by the Americans he was hiding in the bush when he saw Jesus flying overhead in the form of an aeroplane marked with a cross. Jesus then came to him and, as a man, spoke with him and showed him the real Bible. He told Paliau the *Long Story of God*: the story of the creation of the world and of man from the time of the beginning when 'God i stop inside long snow', to the present day. He told of Adam and Eve, of Cain and Abel and of Noah and the Flood. He told Paliau of his own birth to a German white woman called Maria, of how he was killed by the 'Judah government' and he also revealed how this same government had perpetrated a secret deception that deprived the native people of their rightful share of happiness and plenty. Jesus died about three to six generations ago and since that time this government had been trying to 'block his talk' while God had been trying to make it available. God sent the Germans to the Territory of New Guinea, but they treated the people 'like trucks'. He

sent the Australians and the Japanese, but they were also not prepared
to help the people. 'All right,' said God. 'Each one that I tried was
inadequate. They didn't show the real road to Me.' And he turned to
America.

During the Second World War the people had recognized the
Americans as their possible saviours. It was partly because their troops
included so many black soldiers whose presence made it apparent that
the 'way belong native' and the 'way belong white man' didn't need to
be kept separate. At this time, when New Guinea was the centre of the
Pacific campaigns, nearly one million Americans passed through the
area. The people witnessed an enormous display of Western power and
military goods, and, unlike their predecessors, the Americans were not
concerned with establishing their authority and superiority, but instead
they gave freely of their abundant supplies of wealth. For a brief time it
seemed as if a golden age had really arrived and when these benefactors
left and the old administration was re-established, the people felt their
helplessness all the more keenly.

According to the *Long Story of God*, the Americans were still sending
the cargo and still wanted the people to have a share of their wealth, but
the Australians were intercepting the deliveries. To allow justice to be
done the people must prepare themselves and make themselves worthy
of God's attentions. In spite of the visionary source of much of Paliau's
teachings, his instructions were both practical and rational. He wanted
the people to adopt a 'newfella fashion' and to make a break with all the
traditions and ceremonies of the past. There were two waves of inspired
'cargo cults' which sought to speed up the transition from the old to the
new with the help of supernatural agencies. But it was Paliau's call for
developed skills and discipline which finally prevailed, winning him the
respect of the Manus people and of the administration, and earning him
a reputation as one of the most important new leaders to emerge from
the whole Melanesian area.

Jesus told his Apostles all twelve, 'Bring my word everywhere, from
  sunup to sundown. Bring it to every place where God put people.'
  The Apostles heard this from Jesus.
Now all the Apostles wanted to bring the word of Jesus to us. But the
  Judah Government they blocked this talk. The Government said,
  'You cannot bring this message to the native. If you do I will cut
  your throat. Why? Because I have police and soldiers. You must
  obey me. You must alter the Bible book. The real talk of Jesus must
  be left out. You must make it into a different book full of talk-
  pictures to deceive the natives. You missionaries must take that
  book, the real Bible book will stay here.'
Later it happened that Paliau and other men from Manus Island went
  to hide in the bush outside Rabaul, while the Americans were
  bombing the Japanese. Jesus had said to the Americans, 'You must

go. I want to try you America. I have already tried all the other countries. Take my flag, take all this food, and all these ships and go. Never mind Japan, you can defeat them. This flag of mine is the flag of the black men, you will fight under it.'

The Americans came. Jesus came ahead of them. He came as lightning, he came as an aeroplane marked with a cross. He searched over Manus Island looking for a single man whose mind was straight. He saw the village called Mouk. He said, 'It has no land from which to get food or fresh water. It has no rattan. It has no trees for making canoes. It is truly poor, its name is rubbish.' He saw how the people lived, without land, like fish in the water. He felt sorrow for them.

Jesus found Paliau hiding in the bush. He came to him in that plane marked with a cross, to the place where Paliau was hiding, afraid of being hit by the bombs of the Americans.

Jesus appeared to Paliau in the form of an ox. The ox turned into a tall white man with a beard. Paliau was not afraid. They could speak together without making any sound. They went into a house together. There were two chairs, Jesus sat in one, and Paliau sat in the other. The house was filled with a bright light that could be seen from a distance. At the same time they seemed to be surrounded by clouds or smoke.

Jesus showed Paliau a book. It was the real book-tabu, the Bible. It was half metal and half stone and it was encased in concrete. No one could open it and no hack-saw could make a mark on the metal. Jesus said, 'This book, I have put my breath into it. When they want to throw it into the fire, they cannot. When they want to cut it with a hack-saw, they cannot.' This was the knowledge that had been hidden from the natives. Now Paliau was given part of this knowledge.

The Red Man

THE SOUTHERN HIGHLANDERS, Papua New Guinea

One of the first white men seen in this remote highland region was a government officer who arrived on patrol from Ialibu in 1956. This account of his arrival and of his behaviour and attitude towards the people is from the recollections of a man called Tambua Pima who was born about 1931. In 1977 he was interviewed in the Wiru language by Robert Paia, a university student at Boroko in Papua New Guinea.

The 'Wild West Wiru' was the name given to these people by the early missionaries and government patrol officers, and they were famous both for their fierceness and their industriousness. Until 1957 they lived in isolated clan groups, hostile to one another and hemmed in by their fears of sorcery and spirits. This informant's view of the 'bad times of old' and the 'good times' which came with the arrival of the white men, is clearly influenced by the mission attitude to past Wiru history and religion. His natural ambivalence towards the new rulers is revealed in this story of the red man, with his perplexing fluctuations between extremes of friendliness and extremes of violence.

When the red man was at Kumiyane some people went to see him. They took with them their bows and arrows in case of an attack. When they were about fifty yards away they decided to send one spy by the name of Alu to go and observe the camp where this red man was staying. They were confused about his behaviour, but one thing they knew about the red man was that he was a spirit from the sky. After a long discussion they decided to go in groups.

With fear and trembling they started making their way to the camp. When they were about eleven yards away they decided to hide and judge the actions he made. While they were hiding they noticed that he was smoking, so they walked slowly to the camp. It is believed that spirits don't smoke or drink. He came out to greet them and shook hands with them. While they were shaking hands they noticed that his hands were hot. Judging by his clothing people believed that he was both spirit and human. He was so kind to them that he gave them some boxes of matches and in return they gave him some cassowary claws which were their valuable possessions.

At Molo the villagers fled into the thick forest to hide, but some were captured. Red man was so furious with the villagers that he ordered all the woman to strip off their reed aprons and he had sex with them. He got angry with them because those villagers attacked him and most of them left their homes and went into the bushes. There were many villagers who attacked him with his carriers from Kumiyane, but he wounded them and expressed his anger by having sex with those women.

Husbands saw their wives having sex with those foreigners so they started digging a tunnel under the house. The leader of the group told the men to set the house on fire, but it was too late. He saw them coming so he shot them without sympathy. At that time the red man didn't realize that major fights were created when one villager came and raped another villager's wives. Women were restricted when they went to visit their relatives, and those who were caught having sexual intercourse were killed instantly. Sometimes they were so furious that they would cut their wives into bits and pieces. Tigini's wife Madome was among those women who were raped by the red man. After having sex she was released and when she came out of that house she saw her beloved husband lying flat on the ground in his pool of blood. She is still alive today and she said when she recalls those events it reminds her of her poor husband dying like a child in that red man's hands.

When that officer returned to Ialibu he gave the people there some

match boxes, tinned fish, tinned meat and the mirrors. Tinned fish was placed over the fire and it burst out and set the house on fire and caused the cook to lose his eye. The mirror was placed in the men's house and one night Okowane was lighting the fire when he noticed that another Okowane was lighting the fire at the same time. He was terrified, so he reached out to get his axe; and at the same time the other Okowane was reaching for his axe. He wanted to cut the other Okowane, but he realized that he might be cut too. After a pause he cut it with all his force and in the end he found his mirror in many pieces.

A New Dreaming for the Aborigines

THE ABORIGINES, Northern Territory, Australia

In 1887 a Jesuit mission station was established on the Daly River in the Northern Territory of Australia. The missionaries were convinced that if only the Aborigines could be persuaded to become a settled farming people, then they would respond much better to Christianity. They made a large garden and divided it into two parts: one for the mission staff, and one for the sole use of mission Aborigines. A wide variety of vegetables and fruits was grown, along with tobacco. A school was built and lessons begun. Practically, the mission had a tremendous influence on Aboriginal life in the area. It was primarily a haven in which Aborigines could seek refuge. It was also responsible for clearing away certain white persons who had molested Aboriginal women and indiscriminately shot people down. The Aborigines did not welcome the opportunity of becoming farmers. Nevertheless, a small village grew up around this first settlement. The mission suffered many setbacks, with seasonal fluctuations and other hazards. By 1898, conditions had worsened: the Aborigines were becoming restless and there was pilfering and killing of stock. Then came something that happens every few years: after heavy monsoonal rains the great Daly River rose, flooding all the surrounding land – and all their crops were destroyed.

In the following year, the missionaries gave up and departed. By 1945, all that remained of the mission was a single mango tree. But a few older Aborigines still remembered some of the old Christian songs and stories they had been taught.

Maria, whose other name was Mary Christmas, lived by herself. The great Father spoke to her: 'Mary, you have no child. It is better that you have a baby.' That's what the Father said.
This Father, Baiang, is a very big fellow and extremely powerful. He blew a puff of wind towards Mary, and within this breath was the spirit of Jesus. The wind entered Mary and immediately she became pregnant.
Mary grew large with child, and eventually gave birth to Jesus. In one

RIGHT
Around the time of the Second World War many more Europeans penetrated the remote Arnhem Land region in northern Australia. This cave painting from the Wellington Ranges reflects the interest the Aborigines had in the new strangers. The airplane probably belonged to a Salvation Army chaplain who was well known in the area. The four European boats are shown from the outside only, whereas the Macassar prow (top right) is painted in X-ray style because the Aborigines had travelled in these boats.

week he was crawling about on his knees, in two weeks he was walking, and in a month he was a grown man.

Jesus had a large garden in which grew many vegetables and fruits. He watched the apples ripening. He had twelve men to help him. Jesus got his twelve workers to make a long table. When this was done, he set in the middle of it a plate on which rested one apple. The twelve men ate of the apple until they were full. Then Jesus put that apple back on the plate – it had not been completely eaten. Jesus spoke again: 'I gave you one kind of food, an apple. Later I will give you another kind of food.'

They all returned to the garden. Later they grew wheat and made flour. Jesus made a big damper, and when it was ready they all sat down at the long table and ate and ate until they were full. But they could not finish it, so Jesus put the damper away, as he had done with the apple.

And the Father spoke to Jesus: 'All of this is for white men. They will have iron, houses, and everything.' Thus Baiang put motor cars, aeroplanes, houses, horses, and other things for all the white people: and he also made rifles, guns, pannikins and knives. Baiang said to Jesus, 'That is the Dreaming for all the white people'. Jesus was on the side of the white people. He gave all that food and all those things to them. Adam had only native food, for Adam and Riva were Aborigines. They had nothing when they left the big garden owned by the Father.

Chinamen came and grew rice and made grass houses. White men saw the rice and the Chinamen saw the iron houses: the white men saw the rice and the Chinamen saw the flour: each bought from the other. Only the Aborigines had nothing.

Bichiwung Goes to Engiland

THE MAKUSI, Guyana, South America

A religion called Hallelujah is practised today by many of the Carib-speaking Indians of South America. It is a decidedly nationalistic religion which has preserved many of the old gods and rituals of the past, as well as incorporating a lot of Christian teachings.

The missionaries came to the area in the 1860s, and they were received with great enthusiasm. But although the Indians were willing to believe in this new God who lived with his spirit helpers in a sacred place called 'Engiland' they wanted to meet him and talk to him themselves, just as their own shaman priests always made journeys to the other world to speak with the gods there and to obtain advice and guidance from them.

Sometime around the turn of the century a man called Bichiwung was taken to Engiland by a parson. While he was in this magical land he was able to meet God, and as a result of this encounter he 'got' Hallelujah, and brought it back with him. His story is told here, based on accounts which were recorded in the 1950s from adherents of Hallelujah.

At first it seemed unlikely that Bichiwung had been to England, but there is much unexpected evidence suggesting that this really had been the case, including this Hallelujah song:

> Earth Maker God
> is coming
> Mist Maker God
> is coming [5]

for when the people were asked about the nature of God's mist-making they described the low hanging mists which Bichiwung had seen as his boat approached the strange coastline – a phenomenon which had never been seen in Makusi country.

The parson must have promised Bichiwung that he would 'show him God', and when he was shown nothing he decided to make his own private shamanistic journey to heaven. He spoke with God and his suspicions were confirmed, for he learnt how his people were being deceived by the white men, and that from now onwards they must practice Hallelujah which was the only true and modern religion.

When he got home Bichiwung soon made many converts, and he taught them the dances and the songs of his new religion. After his death Hallelujah went into a decline, but it was revived by a man called Abel and subsequently by leaders from other neighbouring tribes, most of whom were already trained as shamans. All the current leaders of Hallelujah maintain the vitality of their faith and their authority over their followers by having regular meetings and conversations not only with God, but with other spirit powers, including Noah and Queen.

> Engiland, Engiland-side my words come
> My words, church, sisters.
> Engiland, Engiland-side Hallelujah comes
> Hallelujah church sisters. [6]

The Makusi people from the Kanuku Mountains were the first to have Hallelujah. A man called Bichiwung and other Makusi men went to work for a parson. They went to his house somewhere behind Georgetown and worked for him and they were taught at his mission school. Now this parson was a white man from England, and he took Bichiwung back with him to England to stay at his home there.

When Bichiwung went to England he saw the sort of cloud which comes low down from the sky. He saw how the skies came down to the sea, and he saw a space in the skies like a door and the steamer went through this door and that was then England. The parson lived there beyond the place where the sky came down to the sea, and he used to teach Bichiwung who began to understand English.

The parson spoke to his relatives about Bichiwung and he listened and understood what was being said. When this white man talked to his family Bichiwung heard him say that he would like to fool this Makusi man he had brought with him, and he was not going to show him God immediately. Bichiwung was told that he could see God if he looked. He looked but he could not find Him.

Eventually the white people told Bichiwung that they wanted to give him some water, and he got a good thing from God and was baptized with boiling water. After this the white people left him alone and went off to other villages. Before going they told him that he must stay in the one place and look after the great wealth that was in it and go nowhere else. Left on his own Bichiwung felt sad and lonely. It was at this time that he saw God and got Hallelujah.

He began to think about all he had been told and he wanted to see God for himself to find out for sure that the white man had told him the truth. He asked some people where he would find God and a trail was pointed out to him leading to a small hill. He went up the hill and prayed and his spirit went to heaven following three boys.

When Bichiwung got to heaven God said, 'What do you want?' Bichiwung said that he had come to see Him, and he wanted to be let in. God let him in and he saw a wonderful garden and he wanted to stay there but God said no, he must go back the way he had come and he must not stay.

Bichiwung told God that he wanted to make sure that he was being told the truth by the white men. God said that the white people were deceiving him and that it was Hallelujah which was good. He said that He had not told the parson the things that he was teaching. He said that the English Bible was left a long time ago and it was now out of date. The Indian Bible was to be the guide for Bichiwung, but he was not to show it to the parson or anyone else and not to use it until he returned home. He was to keep it in his canister. Then God gave Bichiwung a small bottle of white medicine wrapped in paper and this was the Indian Bible. God also gave him some bananas and cassava to plant, and these garden things he took back with him and planted in his garden, so he got plenty of food.

When Bichiwung was speaking to God he saw his wife and children. He wanted to go to them, but God said he mustn't go that way to his wife and children otherwise he would fall down dead. He wanted to go back without passing over the sea, but God said he must go the same way he had come. Then Bichiwung said that he had no money and God told him to borrow from Queen.

Bishiwung returned to the parson's house, taking the things that God had given him and remembering what God had told him about the white man's deceitful teaching and about Hallelujah being good. Through that he left off what the white man had told him and he stopped reading the Bible. Instead he took Hallelujah which he had got on his own, from God.

Bichiwung returned with Hallelujah from England. He also returned with much wealth – a gun and several canisters full of things. When he was back in Georgetown he sent a message to his Makusi friends and relatives asking them to come and fetch all his new possessions and carry them back to his home. He also told them to bring tame parrots, baskets and other things which they could sell in Georgetown and so earn money there to buy trade goods. They did this and obtained much wealth and Bichiwung returned with them.

When he was back with his wife and family Bichiwung began to tell people how he had got Hallelujah and he started teaching it to them. He opened his canister and produced the Indian Bible which God had given to him. The fame of Bichiwung and Hallelujah spread. People came from all parts to visit the Makusi and hear Bichiwung preach and get Hallelujah from him.

Bichiwung's garden had plenty of cassava, plantains, bananas and all the garden produce, and because of this and his knowledge of Hallelujah, bad people became jealous of him. A sorcerer attacked him when he was returning from his garden one day. He died, but his wife took the white medicine he had received from God and she rubbed him with it so that he came back to life again. A second time a sorcerer killed him, and cut him into two or three pieces. His wife gathered the pieces together and smeared the medicine on him and he came back to life. Then they tried to kill him another way: they chopped him up and threw him in the water in pieces so that his wife couldn't find his body to rub the oil on him. Before he died he should have shared this oil so that the people here would have got it.

So Bichiwung died and went to live in heaven. His helpers carried on his work, but the original good Hallelujah words were lost. The people Bichiwung had danced with kept Hallelujah going, but began to forget what he had taught them and they started singing all the old songs and dances, getting them and Hallelujah mixed up.

Then Abel, the founder of Akawaio Hallelujah came, and found the right words and gave people good Hallelujah.

Berebi and the Shivering Poison

THE FORE, Eastern Highlands, Papua New Guinea

The spirits of dead ancestors have a reality of their own. Many examples make it clear that they are believed to exist alongside of human beings. However, they are considered to be powerful and cunning, and easily angered. They may express goodwill, or ill will; they may keep to themselves, or force themselves on people's attention and they are still deeply involved in human affairs. Since they are relatives of the living, they may help or share with them whatever magical wealth they may have.

News of the arrival of the white men also meant news of the arrival of spirits of the dead – since Europeans were usually identified in that way. In the Eastern Highlands, the news took the shape of a cold wind, the Ghost Wind, which blew across the country, bringing with it shivering (*taborabainu*) – that is, people became possessed by the spirit or spirits within the Ghost Wind and began to shiver. This is a manifestation of the Cargo Cult. It can also be induced under certain circumstances. Generally, when possessed, powerful leaders see a spirit and speak with him, performing special rituals, which will cause the spirit to make available much wealth.

Berebi was a man of about sixty-five in 1952, when he spoke about this experience. He had long been a powerful figure – a war leader, a father of many children, and also one who was skilled in dreams, sorcery and magical healing: he was an acknowledged authority on matters relating to spirits. In 1947 he had been taken to the patrol post at Kainantu and met white people for the first time.

Berebi was possessed by shivering when the first Ghost Wind blew southwards in the 1940s. Early in 1948 he had been fighting with members of a neighbouring village. A strange thing happened: his bow broke. He worried about this. Soon afterwards he was visited by several spirits, and so were some of his close relatives. He knew from what he had seen at Kainantu that the white men possessed great wealth. As they were also spirits of local dead, they would naturally wish to share this wealth with their own people. But for this to occur, the correct rituals had to be found. There had to be a 'key' which would open a way for the wealth to come to them.

The story of Berebi is the story of repeated attempts to find the right key. Again and again a spirit appeared and gave instructions. A hole was dug, a house was built, a pig was slaughtered, dances were performed. People waited for a magical transformation to take place, for blood-spattered earth to be filled with pearl-shells, for stones tied up into bundles to become axes, newspaper and salt or other valuable commodities. Nothing happened. It was not the fault of their ancestors, the spirits. It was the fault of the rituals, the instructions had been wrongly interpreted, the key had yet to be found. Berebi was angry: he had not been told clearly enough what he should do. Yet he must bear his humiliation as a personal defeat: 'I am not a child, I am a man, I did as the spirit directed and now I am ashamed before you.'

Berebi was shooting arrows from among heavy pitpit cane, half-way between his own district and a neighbouring one, when he felt two sharp punctures of an arrow in his hand. Looking at his hand, he asked himself, 'What shot me? Did the string of my bow break? Did my own arrow break?' But no, none of these things had happened. As it was only a slight cut, he thought no more about it, and returned home to Ora. This was the time when rumours were rife about the

The circular wooden disc represents the moon. In its centre stands Deuse the creator, holding a wine glass in his right hand. He is surrounded by his possessions which include a boatswain's whistle, a lantern and a telescope.

arrival of white men at Kainantu. It was also the time when the Ghost Wind, that cold spirit wind, was blowing southwards, carrying with it the *Keiginama*, the spirits of the dead.

When he got home, Berebi rested. He rolled some native tobacco and smoked his pipe. As he smoked he began to shiver – first, from inside his belly. Worried, he left his house and cut banana leaves and rubbed his body with them; but the shivering continued.

Men of his lineage group came to him. Seeing him in this state, they said, 'This is no good, we will all die, for this shivering "poison" has come into his skin.' And they all began to cry. Other people also visited Berebi and they, too, said, 'We are frightened of this thing that has come. It's not good that we should die.' Later, they themselves began to shiver.

People brought taro, yams, sugar-cane, sweet potatoes and edible leaves. They made an oven, cooked the food, and distributed it. They asked one another, 'What is this thing that has come among us?' They turned to Berebi and asked, 'What will this thing, this shivering, show to us? What is its meaning for us?' Berebi then offered to show them, if they followed his advice. But first, he said, he would sleep and dream.

After preparing himself by cleansing, he went to sleep and dreamed of the spirit Asigia, a spirit of his own lineage, who appeared to him in the shape of a man with pale skin. He placed in Berebi's hand a piece of red bark, saying: 'Mix this with your tobacco in your pipe. After you have smoked you will shiver. Then you must go to Aburapiti swamp, and after doing what I tell you to do, you will find plenty of shells.' That same night, Berebi scraped some of this bark on to his tobacco, and smoked it. Soon he began to shiver. He went to look for the shells but found nothing. He returned home and slept. Again the spirit came to him and said: 'Collect pig blood and sprinkle the ground at Aburapiti with it, then dig, and you will find shells.' So Berebi took a bamboo container of blood to the swamp and sprinkled it around. He dug and dug, but found nothing.

Some time afterwards, another spirit named Nabuwa came to Berebi as he slept, and told him: 'Leave this place and build another house in the bush. If you do as I tell you, you will find much wealth.' So Berebi sent members of his lineage to build three round houses, which were dedicated to the spirits of the dead by sprinkling blood. Pig meat sprayed with the juice of certain leaves was distributed among the people present. Berebi slept in one of these houses. Nabuwa came to him and said, 'I come to give you axes; I come to give you matches; I come to give you cloth, and I come to give you another thing, and another thing, now you have built me large houses. But first you must sing and dance for me.'

Berebi gave his message to the people. So they came together, and danced and sang before the houses while Berebi sat inside waiting for the gifts. He opened the door of each of the other two houses, but there was nothing inside them. The people became restless and stopped dancing. They said to Berebi, 'All the time we kill pigs for you, but you give us nothing'. And they went away grumbling.

There were recurring periods of shivering. On one occasion, when the Lutheran mission sent an evangelist to Yababi, in Kamano country, Berebi was again possessed with shivering, and Nabuwa visited him as he slept. Nabuwa told him, 'You must not copulate with any woman. If you do, I cannot bring you wealth.' Berebi then built another house at Ora, where he and his family slept and he refrained from sexual intercourse. Again the spirit came to him: 'I come to give you knives, salt and newspaper and other wealth, all of which I will put in this house you have built. But you must do as I direct.'

So Berebi's family returned to their old houses, and he set to work to prepare the new house, as he had been told to do. He placed within it large oven stones, fastened with leaves. The sleeping platform he had made was piled high with these bundles, all ready to be turned into axes. He closed the door and waited. After several days he looked inside, but saw only the stones; there were no axes.

After a while, attention shifted to a woman called Numagia. One of her brothers had died. The spirit of this man entered her belly and she became possessed with shivering. The spirit spoke to her: 'I am Kasajebu, I hold you: I can give you something.' Then the spirit moved from her body to her husband, Asiwa, a half-brother of Berebi. But Asiwa drove it away by hitting his body with branches: and so the spirit returned to Numagia, and told her: 'Later, a big road will come up, and white men will come along this road. You will see them. You remember what I have said. Do not lose this word. And don't stop shivering.' When she woke up, she told her husband: he killed a pig and gave it to her, and she passed it on to Berebi.

Later her husband asked her: 'This spirit who held you, what was he like?' She replied, 'He was my dead brother, but was pale in colour. When he took me walking in the bush, I could see him clearly. His skin was not like ours. Later, he told me, others will come with skin like this.' Afterwards, when Asiwa saw some white men, he said, 'My wife, you have talked true'.

Houses Bulging with Cargo

THE MOUNT HAGEN HIGHLANDERS, Papua New Guinea

The following events took place between 1943 and 1944 in the Mount Hagen Highland region of Papua New Guinea. Twenty-four years later some of the people involved in the movement were asked to explain what happened. This text is based on the accounts of three people: a man who became possessed by the ghost of his ancestors, a man who helped with the building of a cult house, and a boy who was then too young to be directly involved but who had watched and listened. More general details about the movement were given by the man who claimed to be responsible for starting it.

Wealth to these people consisted of shells – pearl shells, cowries, nassa shells, green shells and bailies – and pigs. Stone axes and the salt produced from local mines and springs were also highly valued. People of different clans demonstrated their wealth and therefore their prestige in what was called the *moka* ceremony when all the valuables were set out on show in a great heap and then given away.

The white men penetrated the area in 1933 and by 1939 they had established administrative control. They brought with them quantities of shells, steel axes and other barter goods, and this upset the old order of things for it meant that the clan leaders, the 'big men', no longer necessarily had the greatest amount. It also changed the very nature of wealth, making it cease to be something which was accumulated slowly and painstakingly, but instead something which arrived with great speed in boxes.

It was common in this area for new spirit cults to spread from clan to clan, but years would elapse before a new group adopted an unfamiliar set of rituals. This cargo movement spread in a similar way but it all happened very fast and then it was suddenly over.

One man who lived in the south of the region claimed responsibility for building the first cult house to contain the cargo. After him there were many practical leaders, but the real energy of the movement came from the men who were possessed by the spirits of the dead ancestors. A possessed man sat in the first cult house and he heard the ancestors speaking to him in whistling noises. They told him that a pole must be erected outside the house so that they could climb down to earth. They said that the men who wished for cargo must not have sexual intercourse with their wives, nor must they eat taro, greens or pig's liver. The ancestors said they would bring crates filled with pearl shells, axes, beads and cloth.

The news was carried northwards from one group to the next. The people who had first been in contact with the ancestors gave instructions about preparations for the cargo and they were paid for their information. Certain men in each clan would become possessed and then they too would be able to speak to the ancestors and hear the heavy thudding sound of the boxes landing on the floor of the cult houses.

Then the administration stepped in and burned down the houses and gaoled the leaders. It all stopped as suddenly as it had started, and it was too early for the people to be disillusioned by the failure of the cargo to arrive.

BELOW
Scarlet gates and scarlet crosses have been planted on the ash plains which surround the volcano on the island of Tanna in the New Hebrides. The followers of John Frum believe that many of his invisible men live at the bottom of this crater. The crosses and the gates stand in readiness for the day when these followers emerge from the inferno.

The ghosts sent madness to us. We walked about with them, thinking that they would send us pearl shells, axes and bush knives.

I saw my own ancestors there, holding cargo under their arms in boxes. I saw pearl shells inside the boxes, but when I tried to grasp hold of them the boxes shut and became locked; the ancestors would not give the shells to us.

I climbed tall trees, crawled along their branches and fell down but I was not hurt. Another man looked at me, I looked at him and my eyes and head swam – that was how I became mad. It was as though I had a hot stone turning inside me, making my heart shake and my liver hot and my head felt like water. My proper mind went from me and I spoke strange, crazy words. I made squeaks and screeches like

the white cockatoo bird of the forests.

The Big Man who possessed me with the madness told me that he was
Number One, the *luluai* officer of the ghosts, and he said that he was
now appointing me as Number Two, his boss boy.

And we mad people sat at the ceremonial ground near the cult house
we had built and we sang of how we would court two girls from
among the Sky People. We sang of how the Sky People would come
down and bring us cargo from the sky. We sang:

> Slowly I walk on the road from Kot,
> Slowly I walk on the road from Watek,
> Sky girl Rangent, twist the rope
> For the pearl shell crescent at your neck
> Let us go together.

And in this way we thought of the Sky Girl making a rope from
which to suspend her neck shell, and we sang to her so that she
would bring us cargo wealth.

The government officers had not heard about this thing, nor did the
missionaries know about it. But some of our people, perhaps they
were mission converts, went to the station officer and told him and
he ordered his policemen to visit all the settlements. The policemen
asked the people: 'Have you really seen the ghosts of your ancestors?
Have you really talked with them and eaten with them?' And when
the men said, 'No', it was just some talk that they had heard, then the
government officer was angry and he broke the cult houses and
poured petrol on them and burned them down.

First the officer opened up the cult houses, and he said that there was
nothing inside them. Perhaps there was really nothing inside, but
perhaps the officer found the cargo there and carried it off for
himself. The mad men were all put in prison for six months. Since
this time the spirit has never come back to us. The officer had
chased it away and burned the houses.

Some people told how before the officer came they had seen how the
walls of the cult houses were bulging with cargo. They told that
when the houses were burnt down they cried and rubbed ashes and
dirt on their skin. They were afraid of the officers but they were also
sorry for all the cargo which had been burnt up. They had obeyed all
the proper taboos but their cargo had been destroyed. They said, 'If
the Christians had not reported us we would have got the cargo'.

Tuman and Ambwerk

THE TANGU, North-east Papua New Guinea

> Ambwerk had paper. Tuman had yams and other tubers. Now if it had been the other way round and Ambwerk not Tuman had speared that fish, then you white-skinned people would have had yams, and we black-skinned people would have had paper and all the other good things.[7]

People said that this story about the two brothers should not be told to the white men, especially not to those most official bodies, the missionaries and the administrative officers. Here was the real truth about how the two races were never meant to be rivals, enemies or strangers; for they were in the beginning brothers who were separated from each other because of a series of unforseeable events.

The story of Tuman and Ambwerk belongs within the framework of an old myth and as such it is part of the history of the people. It begins with the ritual murder of a young man who has no father and whose corpse is endowed with supernatural powers; and it ends with an explanation of the invention of aeroplanes, motor boats and all the other good things. The people from the Madang area of Papua New Guinea had been in contact with the white men since about 1900, and it was probably around 1930 when this story emerged in its modern form. The myth-making process which takes unfamiliar events and experiences and incorporates them into a symbolic story is an unconscious and intuitive one. At some point the 'truth' regarding recent historic events is realized, and then the new information becomes at once part of a body of old mythologies which contain the history, the beliefs and the social codes of the people. With their knowledge of Tuman and Ambwerk the people are less afraid of the white men; they have known about their existence all along.

Here it is not only the old times of the past which are explained but there is also an indication of what should take place either in the present or in the immediate future. As a result of some very minor disobedience one of the two brothers kills a fish and precipitates a great flood. It is not always said to be the elder who does this, and the fault is more a chance mistake than a sin. But when the two are separated from each other and the younger one develops all the skills of Western technology, he immediately shows his achievements to his brother who is able to imitate him and acquire the same goods. Four versions of this story were collected and although they all place a slightly different emphasis on the cause of the younger brother's success and the response of the elder one, they all agree that the moral bond of kinship obliges the white men to help their less fortunate brothers by sharing their secrets and explaining the source of their wealth.

One day the men of the village decided to hunt a pig. Duongangwongar, the strange one who had a mother but no father or mother's brother, went with them. When the party had arrived at their meeting place the other men would have nothing to do with him. They told him to go away.

So Duongangwongar wandered off on his own. He saw pig tracks entering a patch of grass, and following these he was confronted almost at once by a pig. Quickly selecting an arrow from his quiver he set it to his bowstring, took aim, and loosed off. The pig was wounded.

Hearing his cries for help the other men ran into the grass, surrounded the pig and killed it with their spears. Then, as each man withdrew his spear from the corpse of the pig he plunged it into Duongangwongar. He fell dead. The men placed his body on a small platform and hid it in the exposed roots of a tree.

When the men returned to the village, Gundakar the mother asked where her son was. They said they did not know, they had not seen him.

That night Gundakar had a dream in which her son appeared to her and told her that he was dead and hidden in the roots of a tree. The next morning she set out to look for his body.

As she walked out of the village, a little bird, the spirit of her son, settled on her shoulders and showed her the path she should take. She found the tree where the body was hidden. She extricated it from the roots and she put it into her string bag and returned to the village. There she collected together some yams, taros, bananas, *mami* and sweet potatoes, put them with the body in the string bag and left the village.

The first village she came to she asked if she might bury her son there, but the villagers refused. The next village refused her and the next, and she travelled on until she came to the coast. She rested by the sea and she came to the village of Dogoi, and there a man copulated with her and there she was able to bury her son. The man Ambwerk helped her. He dug a hole for her, placed the body of her son inside and covered the grave with coconut fronds. Eventually he married Gundakar and she bore him sons.

Meanwhile the body of Duongangwongar rotted in the grave.

One day, when Gundakar was in the village alone and in need of some water she went to the grave of her son. She drew aside the coconut fronds, and, finding salt water and fish coming from the nostrils of the corpse, she filled her pot with water and used it for cooking the evening meal. Her husband and her son thought it good.

That night Gundakar's son grew enormously. Next day when Tuman came to visit Ambwerk, his elder brother, he saw how the boy had grown, and he was surprised. 'Your son has grown so big!' he said to Ambwerk. 'My own sons are still so small – what has happened?'

Nothing was said.

Next day Gundakar collected the skins of her taros, yams and mami and flung them on to the garden. Wonderfully the skins took root and grew back into the soil.

Gundakar returned to the grave of Duongangwongar and collected from his nostrils some water and one small fish which she put in a pot and boiled for her husband and her son to eat.

That night the son grew into a man.

Tuman was so surprised at the transformation that he insisted on knowing how it was done. Gundakar told his wife what to do, 'Go to the grave', she said, 'take away the coconut fronds, draw some water from the nostrils of the corpse, and take one small fish. You

84

LEFT
On the island of Tanna in the New Hebrides there were many stories told about a mysterious messiah figure called John Frum. He first appeared to a gathering of headmen in 1940 and since then he has been expected to return in an airplane bringing a wealth of cargo with him. The Tannese have even constructed airstrips and huge storage sheds in readiness for this event. This shrine portrays John Frum, white-faced and scarlet-coated, with a model of an airplane at his side.

will see there other, larger kinds of fish. Do not take them. Take only one small fish.'

Tuman's wife went to the grave. She removed the coconut fronds and drew some water. In the putrefying nostrils of the corpse she saw a large *ramatska* fish. She speared it.

At once there was a loud rumbling in the earth like thunder. The water from Duongangwongar's nostrils came out in a seething torrent of foam and bubbling waves. And the water, which was the sea, rose up and came between Ambwerk and Tuman. They fled in different directions.

Pondering on the fate of his elder brother, Tuman took a leaf and threw it on the waters. Ambwerk, who had found refuge on high land, saw the floating leaf. He picked it up exclaiming, 'Oh! My younger brother is well. He has sent this leaf to me to find out how I am. So I will send it back to him.' He threw the leaf back in the sea.

Then Tuman saw the leaf and knew that Ambwerk was safe. He took another leaf and writing a message on it he sent it to Ambwerk. Ambwerk received the note and sent an answer in return.

Tuman felled a tree. He hollowed it and made a canoe and set off to visit his elder brother. Ambwerk saw him approaching and wondered what it was. When Tuman had beached his canoe and brought it near the village, Ambwerk looked at it and marvelled. 'Who showed you how to make this?' he said. 'Surely you did not do it all by yourself?'

Tuman said, 'I made it myself. I thought of it on my own.'

When Tuman had gone, Ambwerk made a canoe of his own and went to visit his younger brother. Then he returned to his village content.

Tuman started working on a boat. Having made it and had some practice in it he went to show Ambwerk. Again he told him, 'I invented it myself. And I made it on my own.'

Then Ambwerk, not to be outdone, made a boat for himself, and went in it to see his younger brother. Tuman complimented him on his craftsmanship and he returned to his village content.

Tuman constructed a pinnace. He made an engine, fitted it, practised, and went off to show it to Ambwerk. Ambwerk was dumbfounded. He commenced work on a pinnace at once.

Tuman made a motor car, a motor bike, and a large ship with tall masts and a siren which went 'Whooooooo!' His ship was so big it broke his elder brother's jetty, and they had to secure it by ropes passed around coconut palms.

Tuman made an aeroplane, canned goods, cloth, and all sorts of things. Each time he made something he went to show it to his elder brother. And each time he did so, Ambwerk copied him.

THE RACES OF MAN

I know all kinds of men. First there are my people the Indians; God made them first. Then he made a Frenchman, and then he made a priest. A long time after that came the Boston Men and then came the King George Men. Later came the Black Men, and last God made the Chinaman with a tail. All these are new people. Only the Indians are of the old stock.[1]

(Report of the Bureau of Ethnology 1892–3 by James Mooney)

BEFORE THE TIME OF the white men they said that the land which was their home stood at the centre of the world, and the mountain ranges, the dense jungles and the expanses of ocean were the unmarked borders beyond which lay the chaos of places which had no names, places which could not be imagined.

Before the time of the white men they said that there was only one race. It began perhaps with some enormous First Being from whom all life was created; or a man and a woman emerged out of the ground and mated and produced children; or strange totem animals filled with power wandered over the face of the world and gave their strength to the different family groups. Whatever their origins might be, the people knew that always from the very beginning they had been watched over by the inhabitants of the unseen world; the gods, the spirits, the ancestors, and it was this unremitting attention which gave life its sacred quality and gave a purpose to all the rituals and the facts of human existence. Then from out of that nameless area the white men came.

The people were told that they had been wrong; it was another far distant land – which stood at the centre of the world; and it was an unfamiliar, solitary, white-skinned and white-haired god who had created all living things and who now watched over all human beings. The very existence of these powerful strangers was proof that the old myths of the creation were either entirely wrong or at least incomplete. In order to find a place within the new framework that had presented itself the people had to reassess their mythical history and change or adapt it to account for the white men. The answer to the present predicament of uncertainty must be contained within the past, and a new alliance was needed with the gods and the ancestors so that the people's mythical origins could again be related with the facts of the present moment.

The white men themselves offered the story of Adam and Eve. There was, they said, a man and a woman who lived in a fine place and it was warm with plenty to eat. This place belonged to a god and he told them that they must not taste the fruit of a particular tree.

They disobeyed him and he was furiously angry, declaring that from now onwards they and their children and their children's children, would

know nothing but pain, trouble and sadness. Given such an uncompromising narrative, it was hard for the people to believe that Adam and Eve were also the first parents of the white men who in no way appeared to be damned by the anger of their god. So it was that the story of Adam and Eve and their sin became the story of the first ancestors of the Aborigines who were banished to the Devil-Devil country of the Outback and told that they must live 'like bullocks'. It was the story of the Zulus whom God punished saying that from now onwards they must serve the white men. It was the story of the New Hebrides Islanders whose skin was blackened by the juice from the fruit of the *naavi* tree.

No matter how much the white men might deny it, the god who ruled in that garden when time began and who they said ruled over the world now emerged as an all-powerful controller whose love was partial and somewhat false. His was the voice of relentless authority, of unforgiving judgement, demanding absolute obedience to all of his rules and regulations. He stood as the figurehead for all that the white men represented and often when he appeared in his guise as a distant factory owner or king his only spiritual attribute was indestructible power.

Sometimes it was said that this god was indeed the father of both the races of man, and he had originally loved and showed his love equally to his two sons whose skins were of different colours. In several parts of Africa and Oceania there were already stories which told of two brothers whose quarrelling, rivalry and reconciliations established the basis for many of the social and moral structures of a particular group.

These brothers were the ideal vehicles for expressing the changed conditions of the world, for now it was realized that the elder one was black and the younger one white, and it was because of a sin, an irrevocable mistake, even a chance occurrence, that the black and elder son was deprived of his birthright. An account from Oceania tells how the two were separated in a storm and the younger brother was washed up in the land where manufactured goods were to be found. The Limba people of Sierra Leone tell how the Father had prepared a book for his favoured elder son in which all the secret instructions were written. But in his confusion, or perhaps in his blindness, he gave this priceless gift to the white child. The Amazulus say quite simply that the elder brother was the first to leave his home and enter the world, and he did not know what he should take in order to equip himself for the future. Sometimes, for those who feel themselves most utterly defeated by their new masters, it is said to be the fault of the elder brother – his greed, his stupidity, his basic inadequacy – which brings untold punishment onto his head.

However, these stories of the origin of the two races were not always so heavy with defeatism. Some peoples maintained their certainty of being the first race, declaring that their present humiliations could only be temporary. But such confidence could not last indefinitely in the face of complete control by the white men. It was usually those who were experiencing the early stages of the encounter, whose way of life was not

RIGHT
Mbari mud sculpture showing god of thunder and his wife. This shrine dedicated to Ala the Ibo goddess of earth, is situated at Omugote Orishaeze in Biafra, Nigeria.

88

In Nancowry Harbour on Nancowry Island in the central group of the Nicobar Islands the strange scare-devil figures are seen standing among the raised stilts of the houses. The photograph might have been taken by E. H. Man, the first Assistant Superintendent of the Andaman and Nicobar Islands, who lived there from 1869 until his death in 1929, and made a detailed study of the people and their language.

as yet much altered or threatened, who were able to maintain their separateness and superiority. In the 1920s the Netsilik Eskimos said that these new people, born of the union between a woman and a dog, had the minds of small children and they must be humoured and pacified to prevent them from becoming upset or angry. In the 1930s the Australian Aborigines of the Murngin Tribe told how long ago their dog totem rejected all the goods offered to him by the white man, because neither he, nor the people of that tribe who sprang from him, attached any importance to material possessions. But, if these peoples are still alive today, they have probably come to realize a very different story about how the world and the races of man came into existence.

Gluscap (the Man Made First) and Hadam

THE MICMAC INDIANS, New Brunswick, North America

> Gluscap was a great man and he must have been a good man. Probably he is still living. Whether he is a Frenchman, Englishman or an Indian it would be difficult to say; but inasmuch as he was here before the White men came, he must be an Indian.[2]

With his freckles made out of pieces of inlaid glass, this mask of a red-haired sailor shows a remarkably accurate observation of a typical European face. It was carved by the Haida Indians of the north-west coast of Canada and dates from the mid-nineteenth century.

The first encounter between the Micmac and the white men was in 1534 when the French explorer Jacques Cartier came to Miramichi Bay, or, as he named it, the Bay of Boats, referring to the numerous canoes which clustered around his ship. The rich fishing grounds of Newfoundland attracted men from all over Europe, but it was the French who were the settlers, the colonists and the missionaries. The first Micmac was baptized in 1610 and today all the Micmac people are Roman Catholic.

As a result of such a long history of contact, most of their original beliefs and traditions have either been lost altogether or they have been amalgamated with Christianity and with old French folk customs and superstitions. The sun is no longer worshipped as the creator god and the old ceremonies have been forgotten; the ghost spirit *skadegamutc* has become indistinguishable from the French will-o'-the-wisp. But there is one supernatural figure who has not lost his old identity and that is Gluscap.

In the many stories about Gluscap which still survive today he emerges as the cultural benefactor of the people and their protector. He was not the creator of the world, of animals, or of mankind, but it was he who brought about certain changes to the landscape, to the spirit powers, to the wild animals, so as to make the world more pleasing and less dangerous for his people. In the early days he punished the turtle by making him slow and heavy, and he moved the whale from a small lake into the ocean where he would cause less trouble. In more recent times he has helped the people to fight off the white men and he has been to France and to England in order to speak with the kings there and demonstrate his power. This account tells how Gluscap, the Man-made-first, was created, and how he was given the white-skinned, red-haired Hadam as a companion.

The time that Christ made the world, it was dark, so he made the
  stars. It was not bright enough then, so he made the moon. Brighter,
  but not like the day, he made the sun then. He put his own shadow
  on to the water of the bay, so it would rise into the sky to be the sun.
He made a man then, took the earth and made a man. The earth was
  black, when he got the man to walk, he was dark. This man went
  hunting all the time. He gave him a bow and arrow to shoot with.
One time he saw this man was getting lonesome. He went and made
  another man. He got white clay, and this man was a white man. His
  hair was red.
Man-made-first, God was speaking to him, saying, 'That one is your
  own, he will be with you all the time'. Second-man had a sack, with
  papers in it. He was named Hadam.
They went along. One day they saw an island in the bay. Man-made-
  first would go ahead all the time. He said, 'We'll go out to the
  island'. He walked along on top of the water. He said to the other,
  'Wherever I put my foot, you put your foot'. Second-man said, 'Why
  does he say that? I am just as much of a man as he.' So he put his
  foot down on other places and sank down in the water. Man-made-
  first said, 'You will have to go back now. From the people who
  come from you, sin will come.'
One evening Man-made-first heard somebody talking to him, 'You go
  now and give these people the rules. Tell them how to get along.' If
  the people didn't follow the rules, they would be killed and burnt.

This rather austere couple, dressed in the formal costume of the mid-nineteenth century, are said to be a missionary and his wife. The argillite carving is by the Haida Indians of the Queen Charlotte Islands.

Whenever they saw the new moon they had prayers. What they asked
for, suppose a moose, they would get.

Man-made-first left these people on the island and went to another
place. He found another tribe of people with a different language. He
stayed there again five or six years to give them rules, to show them
how to work and to hunt.

He left them and went to the west. We believe he is living yet in this
world. He'll stand as long as the world stands. The last people he
lived with he told he was not going back to rule them. He told them
that sometime they would get religion.

Macassar White Man and Dog

THE MURNGIN ABORIGINES, Arnhem Land, North-east Australia

For many generations, no one can say exactly how many because nothing
has been left behind, the Aborigines of the Arnhem Land coastal region
were regularly visited by Malay traders from the Spice Islands (the
Moluccas). The Malays persuaded the Aborigines to collect pearls, pearl
shells, tortoise shells, edible sea slugs and sandalwood. These things had
no value for the Aborigines but they were prepared to save them so long
as the work was not too tedious. In return they received dug-out canoes,
rice, molasses, tobacco, gin, cloth, belts, tomahawks, knives and pipes.

However, in spite of this regular contact between the two cultures,
very little in the way of spiritual exchange took place. The Malays were
not concerned with changing the way of life of the Aborigines; they
came simply to do their business transactions. As for the Aborigines,
they did not greatly covet the new tools and technologies offered to them
and they were not interested in changing their old patterns of existence.
They ate the fruit of the tamarind trees which had seeded themselves
along the coast; they ate the rice they were given but did not cultivate it;
and they used the new goods that were provided but made no attempt to
construct their own.

When the Australian Government intervened around the turn of this
century and forbade the Malays to go on with their trading, the Murngin
Aborigines reverted to their old ways and little trace of the exchange
survived. Some people did construct their own dug-out canoes, but
many preferred the simple bark ones; a few Malay words remained in the
names of places and families and a few rituals and songs had been
incorporated, but that was all.

The anthropologist W Lloyd Warner lived among the Murngin for
three years in the late 1920s. He studied their myths, their rituals and the
intricate ceremonial and social systems governing their lives which stood
in sharp contrast to the extreme conservatism of their interest in all
aspects of material culture. He came to the conclusion that these strange
people, whose mystic spiritual life was as strong or even stronger than
their daily existence, were governed by the fact that they were not

RIGHT
*Images from the life of nineteenth-
century colonialists and the
aboriginal people of Australia, are
here juxtaposed in this delicate
silhouette drawing which was
painted with the tip of a feather.*

94

interested in any activity that was not pleasurable. They did not want to be controlled in any way by material possessions, things which demanded regular care and attention. They were most happy with goods which were either disposable or which disintegrated of their own accord, like their bark canoes which lasted just for a single voyage.

This story of the origin of the white men and the black men is set in Wongar time, the mythological age of the beginning when the world was inhabited by the totem ancestors, some in the form of animals, some in the form of men. The Macassar White Man in this story is an amalgam of a Malay trader, a European and a mythological being; and the Dog is a totem ancestor of the Murngin tribe. There might be a slight note of regret at how utterly the dog rejected all the things offered to him, but it is only regret and not remorse.

The Wongar Dog always stayed close to the Macassar Man when they
    were in this country. That Macassar Man said to him, 'What do you
    keep your head down for?'
The Dog mumbled the same words as the master.
The master said, 'I am sorry'.
The Dog said, 'I am sorry'.
The master of the Dog said, 'What do you want? Do you want
    something?'
Dog replied, 'What do you want? Do you want something?' He
    imitated his master's speech.

LEFT
Repoussé aluminium panel showing Adam and Eve and the serpent. It was made by a contemporary Nigerian artist called Ashiru Olatunde from the Oshogbo region in Nigeria.

The Macassar Man said, 'I am going to give you tobacco, tomahawks and canoes, and all the things my people have'.

The Dog replied, 'No, I don't want them'.

The Macassar Man offered the Dog a match, the Dog said, 'O, no, I have fire sticks'.

The Macassar Man said, 'All right then. You are going to become a black fellow. I will give you nothing. I'll be a Macassar Man and I will keep all these things. You get off that mat and sit on the ground!'

The Macassar Man built houses with posts to give to the Dog. The Dog refused them so the Macassar Man picked up his houses and went away.

After the Dog had refused all the things that the Macassar Man possessed, the Man said, 'Why do you act like this?'

The Dog replied, 'It is because I want you to be a Macassar Man. I am a black man. If I get all these things then I will become a white man and you will become a black man.'

The Dog went to Elcho Island, and when he got to the Cadell Straits he made a bark canoe to get across. After making the canoe he put it in the water but it sank. The Dog sat down and looked at it. He could do nothing. He was defeated. He sat down on the beach and his canoe turned into stone under the water, and he also turned into stone. The name of this time a long time ago was Wongar time. It happened when the world started.

And now, when we see the water break on that stone which is Dog and his canoe, we think about all this, and we know why the black men have so little and the Macassar Man and the white men have so much.

UThixo and Adam and Eve

THE BANTU, *Pondoland, South Africa*

Pondoland is a rugged strip of coastline near Natal in South Africa. It was the last block of territory to be colonized and was finally annexed by the British in 1894.

In the 1930s when this story was collected, there was still a big division between the Bantu who were 'dressed people' and had adopted as much as they could of European culture, and those who held on to traditional dress and custom. However, in spite of this division the two ways of life inevitably had a strong effect on each other.

God, whose name is uThixo, seems to be a new concept for the people, and yet his presence is accepted by the converted and the unconverted. A man who had been under no direct mission influence declared, 'Those who die become amathongo and go to live with uThixo. Those who are wicked go to uSathana and never become amathongo.'[3] These amathongo are the spirits of the dead ancestors who remain very concerned with what is happening in the land of the living. At times they are hungry and want to eat, and then cattle are ritually slaughtered for them. If they are not treated with the correct deference, they become angry and cause sickness, trouble and death. The people say, 'The amathongo are like the Government, they like him have never been seen'.[4]

This story is a modern adaptation of an old myth, common throughout southern Africa, which tells of two animals, usually a chameleon and and a lizard, and the origins of death.

The white people were not created here, they came across the water in ships. UThixo created two people here, Adam and Eva. They were the black people. He put them in a garden where they could eat everything except the fruit of a big tree.

Chameleon was sent by uThixo to tell them that they could live without working. Then uSathana said to Lizard, 'Hurry up and tell people to eat of that tree'.

The people in the garden listened to Lizard. Eva ate first. Then uThixo said, 'For your sins white men will be your masters and you will have to work to live. You, woman, will have to suffer by bearing children. They will no longer be created my way but they will come through connection with man, and with great pain and labour. You both will have to work and live by the sweat of your brow.'

Later Chameleon was sent by uThixo to come to earth and say, 'People are not to die'. Lizard heard this and he ran in a great hurry and said, 'People are to die day by day'. And so when Chameleon arrived and said, 'UThixo says people are not to die', the people answered, 'The first news that came with Lizard is already written in the books, you come too late'.

So people have been dying ever since that time.

BELOW
A decorative argillite plaque showing two men, a woman and a dog who seem to be on a boat. It was made by the Haida Indians of the north-west coast and probably dates from the end of the nineteenth century.

The Shawnee Indians and the Master of Life

THE SHAWNEE INDIANS, Ohio and Pennsylvania, North America

The Shawnee Indians were a small, nomadic and warlike tribe whose hunting bands were used to ranging enormous distances all over the eastern states of America. Throughout the eighteenth century, they and their allies the Wyandots and the Delawares were in a state of constant guerilla warfare with the advancing forces of the white settlers who steadily penetrated and occupied their rich hunting grounds.

During the American War of Independence they sided with the British forces and their utter defeat was finalized when, under the Treaty of Greenville in 1795, they sold and signed away most of their territorial rights. They were left in a state of brooding discontent, deprived of almost all the symbols of their self respect. Around this time a new myth concerning the origin of the white men and the Indians became current. It was said that the Shawnees were originally the superior race but, because they had become corrupt, the Great Spirit had decided to punish them by sending the white men to their land. But such a harsh punishment could not be indefinite and soon the time for revenge would come. This version of the myth was told by a Shawnee chief at a convention held in Fort Wayne in 1803.

The Master of Life, who was himself an Indian, made the Shawnees before any other of the human race; and they sprang from his brain. He gave them all the knowledge he himself possessed and placed them upon the great island, and all the other red people are

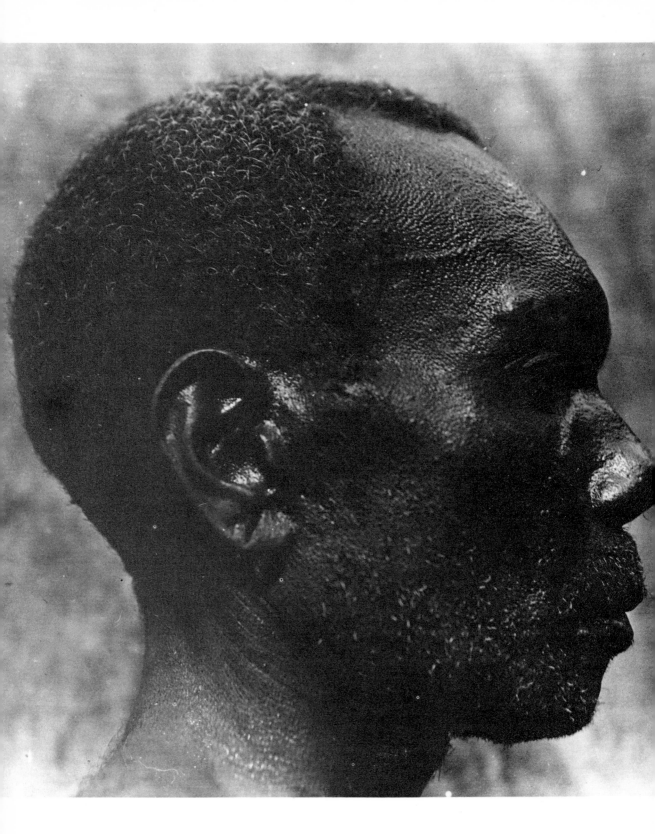

descended from the Shawnees.

After he had made the Shawnees, the Master of Life made the French and the English out of his breast, the Dutch out of his feet and the long knives out of his hands. All these inferior races of men he made white, and he placed them beyond the Stinking Lake, which is now called the Atlantic Ocean.

The Shawnees for many ages continued to be masters of the continent, and they used the knowledge they had received from the Great Spirit in such a manner as to be pleasing to him and to secure their own happiness. However, after a great length of time, they became corrupt, and the Master of Life told them that he would take away from them the knowledge that they possessed and give it to the white people. He said that he would restore this knowledge to them when, by a return to the good principle, they again deserved it.

Many ages after that, they saw something white approaching their shores. At first they took it for a great bird, but they soon found it to be a monstrous canoe, filled with the very same people who had got the knowledge which belonged to the Shawnees.

After these white people had landed they were not content with having the knowledge which belonged to the Shawnees, but they also stole their lands from them. They even pretended to have bought these lands, but the goods that they exchanged for them were more the property of the Indians than of the white people, because the knowledge which enabled them to manufacture these goods actually belonged to the Shawnees.

But all these things will soon have an end. The Master of Life is about to restore to the Shawnees both their knowledge and their rights, and he will trample the long knives under his feet.

Why Men Became Black

THE MALEKULA ISLANDERS, New Hebrides

Bernard Deacon arrived in South West Bay on Malekula Island on 21 January 1926. He spent a little over a year there making anthropological studies of the people, and then, just as he was planning his departure, he caught blackwater fever and died. His notes, later compiled as a book, are a record of a people in the process of being destroyed both mentally and physically before anyone had the opportunity to observe how they lived. This has happened many times to many peoples, but it is only occasionally that there is someone there to witness it and communicate what he sees. In a letter Deacon wrote, 'The death-rate here is terrific. Work is largely a race between speed of note-taking and speed of diffusion of epidemics. The whole of Malekula is convinced it will soon die out, and I'm inclined to think it's right.'[5] Or again, 'I was asking for skulls the other week and received the ironic reply, "In a little while the white men will be able to take all of ours"'.[6]

There was wave upon wave of sickness: measles, consumption, influenza, whooping cough and dysentry, which wiped out whole villages and drove the few survivors to the coastal regions. There was also the loss of the spiritual life which undermined any desire to survive. Deacon met the last man able to conduct a ceremony which had always been held every four years in order to ensure that the vital energy and strength of the district would endure. Often the few informants who could remember the old laws, rituals and myths would be dead before they had told him all that they wished to say.

In common with so many people of the Pacific and elsewhere, the Malekulans of the south-west area where this story comes from had a belief in a mythical race of white-skinned, narrow-nosed beings, sometimes represented as one single white-skinned hero-god, to whom they gave the name Ambat. It was these beings from a past time who were responsible for all the cultural advances on the island, whether it was the acquisition of a certain skill or the existence of some natural phenomenon such as the sacred standing stones. And all the troubles of the world had descended upon the people when they were left alone. It meant that the white men were welcomed, as they so often were, as the returning heroes come to bring back another golden age. It also meant that although the story of why men became black must have been influenced by the Adam and Eve of the missionaries, it could be based on an earlier myth in which the two first people were punished for their disobedience by being given a blackened skin.

He-Abides-By-Himself had children two, man one and girl one. They lived in that village called Leneven. And Father he said, 'You-two shall eat trees many, and the one tree you-two shall not eat. It is the *naavi* tree.'
And Father spoke, 'Finish', and Father he left them-two. He went into a desert place.
And Old Man he came to them-two. He said, 'For what is it you-two shall not eat tree this?'
They-two said to Old Man, 'Father he said we-two shall not eat'.
Old Man said, 'Father he lied to you-two. A tree that is good is this tree here. You-two shall eat and you-two shall know all things like Father.'
And they-two said, 'Father said, "You-two shall eat and you-two shall die"'.
Old Man said, 'You-two shall not die'.
And the woman she took the fruit of the naavi tree and she ate. And she said to her brother, 'Truly, this tree is sweet'. She gave to her brother and he ate. And the juice of the naavi tree ran down their breast.
Then they-two looked but saw not Old Man. They-two spoke, 'Old Man, he went where?'

RIGHT
Images of canoes and European ships, white traders and Eskimo hunters, reindeer seals and whales are painted in black on a sealskin. The skin was obtained by the captain of an Arctic whaler from the Chuckchi Eskimos of the Bering Straits, at the end of the nineteenth century.

The woman she said to her brother, 'The juice of the tree is black'.
She said, 'We-two will go into the water, we-two will wash the black
juice away'. And they-two went into the water and they-two washed,
but it did not finish.
Then they-two were afraid of Father. They-two said, 'Father will come
and kill us-two, we-two did not believe him'. And they-two ran and
lived in the desert place.
Father came and looked for them-two and he saw not them-two. He
called out and them-two answered. Father said, 'For what you-two
did not stop in the house?'
The man he said, 'We-two were bad'.
Father said, 'For what you-two were bad?'
The man said, 'Old Man come to us-two and spoke and we-two ate the
fruit of the naavi tree'.
Father his head was bad. He said to them-two, 'You-two believed Old
Man, and you-two hated commandment mine, and it was as if you-
two hated me. Now you-two shall work for Old Man who made
you-two eat tree that was bad.
'You-two shall come. We together will pull the canoe to the water,
and I say goodbye to you-two, and I am going to leave you.'
And they-two cried.

The Woman Who Mated with a Dog

THE NETSILIK ESKIMOS, Arctic Canada, North America

According to the Netsilik Eskimos of the Boothia Peninsula Nuliajuk is
the mistress of the sea and the land. She is the mother of all beasts and she
also has a special hold over human beings and is greatly feared by them.
She lives on the bottom of the sea in a house built inside a bubble and the
entrance is guarded by a fierce black dog. If Nuliajuk is angry she hides
all the animals and the people must starve until she again feels merciful
towards them.

One version of this story tells how a group of men, women and children
set out on a raft to go hunting. Nuliajuk was a little girl who nobody
loved or claimed as their own, and they intended to leave her behind.
When she climbed onto the raft they seized her and threw her into the
water and when she tried to grab hold of the sides of the raft they cut off
all her fingers. She sank to the bottom of the sea where she became the
great sea spirit and her amputated fingers were transformed into seals.
Because the people had despised her and treated her so cruelly when she
was a helpless child she was endowed with a terrible power over the
world of men.

However, there are some who say that this Nuliajuk is the same person
as the woman who married a dog and whose offspring were the white
men and the Indians. They say that this woman was so ashamed at having
participated in the murder of her father that she allowed herself to sink to

the bottom of the sea, and the black dog who now watches over her is the one who was married to her.

The story goes that a father one day in anger said this to his daughter, 'You won't have a husband, I wish you had a dog for a husband'.
When evening came and they had lain down to sleep, the man's dog came in, but in human form. He wore a dog's tooth on his breast as an amulet.
As soon as the others had fallen asleep he lay down beside the girl and embraced her, and then he hung fast with her and dragged her out into the entrance passage. In that way they became man and wife.
The woman became pregnant, and when she had got a big stomach and would soon be confined, her father rowed her over to an island, as he did not want the trouble of the children she was going to have.
On the island the woman gave birth to a litter of young that later were to become the white men and the Indians.
The father, it is said, used to go to them in his kayak and take meat to them.
But when the children were grown up the woman said to them one day, 'Your grandfather was not so wise that time he wanted me to have a dog for a husband. Throw yourself upon him when he next brings you food.'
The story goes that the girl's young started to lick the kayak for the blood the next time the father came with meat, and then they threw themselves upon him and tore him to pieces.
After that the woman sent her young out into the world. To those who were to become Indians she gave her inner shoes to use as boats. Then she let them go away, saying that they were to be hostile to all men.
But to those who were to be whites she told them to be of a friendly disposition, and set them out in her outer shoes. These were to be their ships.
But when she tried to go on board to them, these children threw her into the water. She seized hold of the edge of the boat, but they chopped off the third joint of her fingers. After a little while these came up as seals.
Again the mother got hold of the edge of the boat, but they chopped off the next joint of her fingers. It was a little while before anything came up out of the water, and then her finger joints came up as bearded seals. Again she caught hold of the boat and again they chopped a joint off her fingers. It was some time before anything came up, and then they came up as walruses.
After that the woman sank to the bottom of the sea where she became Nuliajuk, the mother of the beasts.

We Thought We Possessed All Things

THE AMAZULU, South Africa

The Reverend Callaway was a British missionary who lived with the Amazulu from 1854 until the late 1870s. He was inspired by a determination to record the legends and beliefs of these people, not in the usual Europeanized manner, but keeping as close as possible to the narrative style of the speaker. He worked from dictations which he first wrote down in the original dialect and then translated literally into English. He gave the name of the man or the woman who came to speak to him and he included everything, the repetitions, the uncertainties, the interjections from others who were present. The result is a collection of documents which speak with that halting poetic style of true oral literature.

Callaway questioned the people in great detail about their beliefs in the gods and the origin of the human race. Everyone agreed that Unkulunkulu was the first man, and he was born out of a bed of reeds, 'We heard it say Unkulunkulu sprang from a bed of reeds. There first appeared a man who was followed by a woman. Both were named Unkulunkulu. The man said, "You see us, we sprang from a bed of reeds", speaking to the people who came into being after him.'[7] Then there was also Uthlanga – the word means literally a reed that is fully grown and can produce offshoots – and it was this many-coloured god who was the source of all life. But although the substance of these myths remained constant, Callaway, and presumably the other missionaries before him, produced terrible confusion and uncertainty by their persistence in asking questions which had no answers, questions which had never needed to be asked before. He wanted to know whether Unkulunkulu had died or whether he lived for ever. He wanted to know where Uthlanga was to be found; he wanted to be shown the bed of reeds.

From some came apologetic denials, 'We do not understand the account of Unkulunkulu, it is not easy to understand, it is mere fable. Our fathers who are dead died without knowing the country where Unkulunkulu created man that he might have life. And the old people who are still living do not say that they know the country where he created men.'[8] Others expressed their confusion. 'Her son said, "No, yesterday she said to the missionaries that Unkulunkulu was from beneath. But now she says he was from above." And the woman said, "Yes, yes, he went up to heaven afterwards. Truly Unkulunkulu is he who is in heaven. And the white men they are the lords who made all things."'[9] Always there is the fact that these people who thought themselves to be content, to be strong, who thought that they 'possessed all things' had to confront the shock of their defeat. The story given here is an explanation of the mistake which took place in the beginning, the simple mistake which resulted in this terrible defeat.

Uthlanga was of many colours. They say, 'He was white on one side and on the other black, and another side he was covered with bush'.

RIGHT
A white man and his wife in early nineteenth-century costume are painted on a rock shelter in the Rouxville district of the Orange Free State in South Africa. The Bushman artist was probably depicting members of one of the first Dutch settler groups which came to the area at that time.

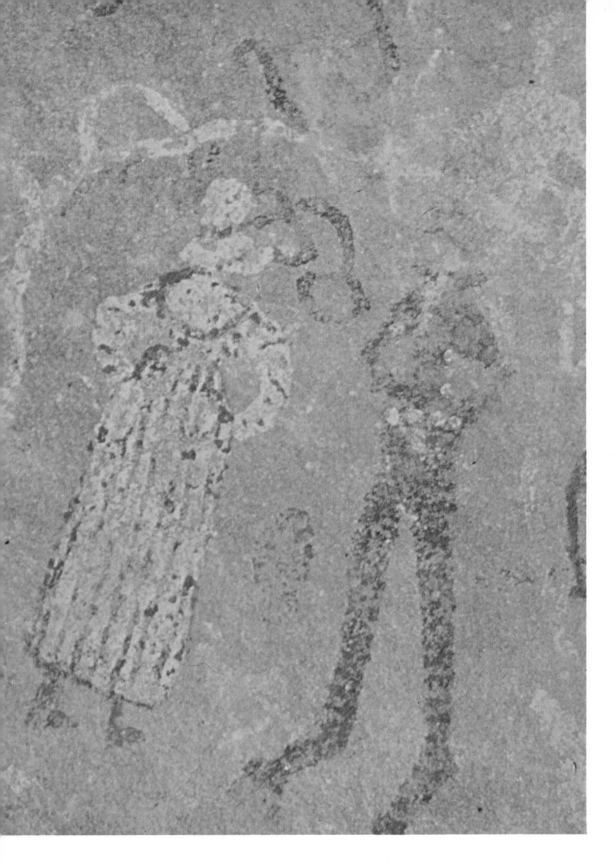

So we say, 'Perhaps they spoke of the hairiness of his body and so called it bush'.

It is as though we sprang from Uthlanga; we do not know where we were made. We black men had the same origin as you white men. But we black men at our origin were given cattle, and picks for digging with the arms, and weapons of war. It was said, 'It is enough, you must now make do for yourselves'. So we departed and came in this direction. You white men stayed behind with all the good things and with laws also which we did not possess.

We used to hear it say by our fathers, they too having heard it from others, that a man first came into being, and then a woman after him. After that a cow came into being, it appeared walking with a bull. After that a female dog, and after her a male dog; and after that all the little animals, and elephants; all came into being in pairs.

After that corn came into being. When the corn was ripe the man said to the woman, 'That which you now see is something for us to eat. We shall eat at once.'

So we came out possessing the things which we needed and thinking that we possessed all things, and thinking that we were wise and that there was nothing we did not know. We lived by boasting that we possessed all things.

But now the white men have come here with their wagons. Oxen are

108

yoked, the people are clothed in fine linen, and they are doing things
which we thought could not be done by man; things we did not
think could be of any use to us. We did not know the ox is useful for
many purposes. We used to say, 'The purpose of the cow is that it
have calves, and we eat milk, and the purpose of the ox is that we
should kill it and eat flesh', and that was all. We knew no other
purpose of cattle. When one is killed we prepare its skin and make
women's clothes and blankets, and that is the whole purpose of the
ox. We wondered when we saw oxen yoked to a wagon with goods
in it, and we saw it go through the land and go for a long distance
and there being nothing that is not in the wagon. And when the oxen
are loosened and all the property of those men comes out we said,
'Those people are coming who go about with a house'.

We saw that we black men came out without a single thing, we came
out naked, we left everything behind because we came out first. We
came out in a hurry and they waited for all things that they might not
leave anything behind.

As to their victory over us, they were not victorious by armies, they
were victorious by sitting still – they sitting still and we also sitting
still. We were overcome by their works which made us wonder and
say, 'It is not right that we should think of fighting with men who
can do such things'.

It was as if because their works conquered us their weapons would be
bound to conquer us also.

Kanu and the Book

THE LIMBA, Sierra Leone, West Africa

The anthropologist Ruth Finnegan collected the story of Kanu and the
Book in 1961. She tells how she had once narrated the basic plot of
Adam and Eve, only to hear it retold two years later transformed into a
traditional tale explaining the reason why there is such hatred between
the *bankiboro* snake and men; why life is so difficult for the Limba; and
the bad things which result when a woman favours her lover more than
her husband – Ifu's lover was the long, red-spotted bankiboro snake and
they had gone 'far in that love' and it was on his advice that she broke the
prohibition and ate the red-coloured fruit.

The story told here is obviously influenced by the Old Testament
account of Jacob and Esau, with its theme of a lost birthright, but it has
a different moral weight put upon it which is based on the Limba concept
of *yanfa*. It is considered very wrong and dangerous to slander someone,
to speak behind his back, to show a secret preference for one person
above another, and it is said that when such yanfa is committed it will
result in the one who is slandered being the winner, and the slanderer
being the victim of his own abuse. And that is the pattern of events here
when a crucial mistake of identity deprives the favoured black brother

of the book for all knowledge which his father has prepared especially for him.

At that time a man bore two children. Well, these two children, one had a white body, the other he was born with a black body. These two people, Kanu the Father made them, these two people he put them down on the earth. They lived there both of them in the world. The parents had the two children. One was white, one black. But they were full brothers, one mother, one father.

But this child – his mother she loved the European, the white one. That pleased her. Now the black one – his father loved the black one.

Well, one day, the father said, 'Let us leave the earth. Let us see what the children will do on the earth. But one day I will tell you, we will see what the children are doing on the earth, if they are hearing what we told them.' That was their father.

He made a book. He wrote everything, how to make a ship, aeroplane, money, how to make everything. He wrote it in the book to help the one he loved. He too, he took and made a hoe, he made a cutlass, he looked for millet, he made groundnuts, he made pepper, he made a garden, oranges, everything. He put them down, he gathered them into a pile. He took the hoe, he took the cutlass, he put them down there.

At that time, well, the man said, 'We will hide now, I with you, to see what the children will do'. Then the wife said, 'What will we leave for the children?' He said, 'No, I have got my plan'. He was the one who married the woman, he the man. Behold, he was wanting to act unfairly. He was going to take the book, to give it to the black one, he the father. He wanted to give the book to the black one. The mother wanted to give it to the European, the white one, to give him the book. She said, 'What will we do?' He said, 'We will bring what we are leaving for the children'.

Now their father he could not see well. He could not see the children clearly. He said, 'Child, you, when you go to hunt, do not go very far'. He the child, just turned round, he caught a sheep, he killed it. He, the white one came, he said, 'Father, I have brought meat. I went to hunt for it.'

Well, that pleased the father. Because he could not see well, he thought he was lifting down the hoe to give the white one. Behold it was the book he took. 'Take the book for me.' The wife took the book. He said, 'Give it to the child, the one who brought the meat'. He was given the book. He was not afraid to peep at it. He started reading it. He started seeing the things, how to make an aeroplane, how to make everything, how to make a ship, he saw it in the book.

The black one came. He said, 'Father, greetings. What have you kept for me? I have killed a bird. It is what I have brought.' He said, 'Ah, my child, you are left as a foolish man. Well, take this hoe. Here is a

RIGHT
A dignified man intent on studying a book is believed to be the portrait of a Swedish or Swiss missionary. It was carved from the wood of the silk cotton tree, and dates from the mid-nineteenth century (Congo).

basket, rice is in it. Millet is in it. Groundnuts are in it. Everything
that you use when you go to work is there. But you are likely always
to be left behind. He is more than you. Everything, if you want to
get it, you have to ask your companion, the white one.'
You see us, the black people, we are left in suffering. The unfairness
of our birth makes us remain in suffering. Our mother did not love
us. She loved the white people. She gave him the book. There they
saw how to make everything without suffering.
This is the way. Yesterday we were full brothers with them. We come
from one descent, the same mother, the same father, but the
unfairness of our birth, that is why we are different. We will not
know what you know unless we learn from you. We are brothers of
the same parents, that is why you learn from books, to teach us black
people so that we may know. Why we are alike – we are full
brothers.

All People Come from the Same Place

THE MERU, Kenya, East Africa

The Meru are a Bantu tribe who mostly inhabit the Central Province of
Kenya. In common with many of the Bantu peoples, they say that they
came originally from a different, distant place, and they have many
legends which tell how, a long time ago, they left a land in the north
which lay beyond a great stretch of water. They call this place Mbwa and
they say that it was a rich and fertile land although they themselves were
not able to enjoy its pleasures for they were kept as slaves there, ruled
over by a powerful people called the 'red-clothed ones'.

Now it happened once that these overlords decided to set the Meru
three very difficult tests. They succeeded in the first two, but they
were unable to forge a spear that 'when fixed on the ground, could reach
the sky'. Rather than face a cruel punishment, their leader decided that
they must escape. They could not take the old people with them, and so
they collected a heap of dried cattle dung for them to burn. Then all those
who were fit and well gathered together and set off for the south. They
came to a great expanse of water, the 'red sea', and by this time their
enemies were close behind them. But their leader called on God to help
him and his people and when he struck the water with his staff, the water
divided and a way was opened up. Everybody reached the other side in
safety and they found themselves in a place where they were indeed their
own masters, but this land was barren and harsh and it offered nothing
of the easy opulence of the lost land of Mbwa.

It must have happened that when the Meru told the missionaries about
their historic migration, the missionaries answered with the story of
Moses and the Children of Israel so that the two themes became inter-
twined. In the version included here fragments of the old and the new
have been combined in such a disjointed and reduced form that they

often seem incomprehensible unless one knows the model on which they were based.

Another complication here is that the story has moved into a third stage. The land of Mbwa has become the rich land of the white men, who, it seems, were so determined to chase and capture their escaped slaves in order to make them suffer that they set about inventing planes and boats in their rich land so that they could cross over the great water without the benevolent intervention of a god.

All people come from the same place. But the first to be born was a
  black man, and after him a white man was born. Then they started
  quarrelling as two brothers quarrel.
A girl was also born. Her name was Bong'ina, which means Of-the-
  Mother. It was because of her that they started quarrelling.
A black man shouted, 'We shall go away!' And they heard it, 'We
  shall go away!' and they all said, 'Now we go away!'
Some warriors were sent out to look where to cross over to the other
  side of the red sea.
They stayed away for many days. They lighted fires and having seen
  that they said, 'Let us forge a spear'. They came back and they said,
  'We did not find a crossing', and then they went off again.
But God said to them, 'Go, because I want to speak to you'. God
  came. God stroked the water with his staff and the red sea divided.
  And that was how we passed through the water. There have been
  men who came and asked us, 'How could you pass through that
  water?' and that was how.
Now, these are the names by which the people were called afterwards:
  black, white and red. Those who crossed during the night are called
  the black ones; those who crossed at dawn were called the red ones;
  those who crossed when the sun was up were called the white ones.
  And the water closed up again.
We arrived here, we came here. We did not have any of the troubles
  we had before we left.
When the white men in the land of Mbwa were by themselves they
  started making all the things that you see. They made boats, planes
  and the other things which they used in order to come here to our
  land. Now that they have come here there is nothing that they cannot
  do. And now we suffer.
But God knows that we two came out together from the same place.
  Look, I spit on the ground, in my saliva there are some dark water
  parts and there are some white parts, but all comes from the same
  place.
That is to show that we should not be divided. All of us are one.
  All are one.

Adam and Riva in Devil-Devil Country

THE ABORIGINES, Northern Territory, Australia

This account, like 'A New Dreaming for the Aborigines', is another·
survivor of the brief encounter between the Aborigines of the Northern
Territory of Australia and a Jesuit Mission which tried, unsuccessfully,
to convert them and establish a simple farming community in the 1880s.

The Great Father said: 'I haven't a son. It is better that I should have
a boy.' So he made Adam, by blowing a breath of air. Adam lived on
the earth and cultivated tomatoes and apples. He had been shown
how to do this by the Father, who lived in the sky.

One day the Father spoke to his son: 'Adam, you have no woman,
have you?' 'Yes Father, I have no woman, but no matter, I work by
myself as an unmarried man.' 'Ah, you must take a woman,' the
Father insisted. 'How can I take one? There are no women here.'
'Ah, I will get you married. You stand up there, Adam,' the Father
said.

So Adam came to that place and stood up. 'What shall I do?' 'You
just stand up there, and I will get you married,' repeated the Father.
Adam thought to himself, 'And where is there a woman? There is no
woman here, only myself.'

Now the Father made a puff of wind come from his mouth, and a
woman stood beside Adam. 'Ah, there's a woman here, Father!' This
was Riva. 'Yes, you may have that one,' replied the Father. 'But you
must not sell her to any white man, nor to any Chinese, Malay,
Japanese or Aboriginal. You must keep her for your own. She
belongs to you, yourself.' That's what the Father said.

'All right, Father,' said Adam. 'And you mustn't steal, or take another
woman. You mustn't kill women, mustn't kill anyone,' the Father
continued. 'All right, Father,' Adam promised.

After a time, the woman made Adam go wrong. It happened this way.

Adam and Riva were living together, and each day they worked in
their garden. Now the apples ripened and Riva saw them. 'Adam,'
she said, 'that fruit is ripe. We had better eat.'

'No,' replied her husband, 'Baiang, Father, will see us.'

'It doesn't matter, Baiang is a long way away.'

'But Baiang said, "Don't steal them". He will see us. Baiang always
looks on us.'

Adam was all right at first. However, at last he was persuaded to pick
one apple. Breaking it open, the two began to eat.

Now Father looked, saw them. He called them to him. So Adam and
Riva came. Then the Father spoke: 'Adam, come here! You two
married people! What did I say to you before, Adam? "You mustn't
sell women, mustn't kill women, mustn't steal." That's what I said.
Why have you eaten an apple? You are finished with this place here.
You must go away. You must go to where there are yams, lilies,

goanna, bandicoot, snake, kangaroo, wallaby, fish. That is what you
will eat now. No more may you eat my food – you must go like a
horse, like a bullock!' Thus the Father spoke in anger, hunting them
away from the big garden and into the Bush.

And so Adam and Riva, who were of the same skin colouring as the
Ngulugwonggu people, came to live in the Bush as Aborigines,
hunting and collecting food, no longer watched over by Baiang.

If Adam and Riva had not eaten that apple, we Aborigines would have
lived like Chinese or white people. We would have had the good
food. But we went wrong, and so we collect and hunt for our food.
Adam talked wrongly; he stole that apple belonging to Baiang. This
made him no good! And it is from Adam and Riva that all of us
came. Adam could not stay with the great Baiang. Instead, he went
to Anmel, to Devil-Devil country. Adam was a bad man. The big
garden he and Riva had worked in belonged to the Father. Adam was
only the gardener.

Now, if you commit adultery with a woman, kill men and women, or
steal food from anyone, from a white man or a Chinese – then
Baiang will dislike you, and will send you to Anmel. If you don't do
these things, Baiang will take you to a very good place when you die.
Father always sees everything: and if you are bad, he will say,
'Better I should kill him, or get someone else to kill him'.

The Indian Who Danced

THE PUEBLO INDIANS, New Mexico, North America

The Pueblo Indians live communally in adobe villages in much the same
way as they did a thousand years ago. They still farm the same basic crop
of corn and melon and dance the same dances in honour of the sacred
spirits of rain and fertility to ensure that their work is successful. In spite
of their Christianization by the Spanish in the eighteenth century and in
spite of their incorporation into the United States of America in the
nineteenth century, they have managed to maintain their ancient religious
beliefs and rules of social government with a defiant tenacity.

It was the eastern Pueblos who came most strongly under the influ-
ences of the Jesuit priests in the eighteenth century because they were
living along the Rio Grande Valley within easy access to the then newly
established Spanish capital of Santa Fe. However, although the old
dances and forms of worship were banned, the inspiration which lay
behind them was not lost and often they survived unchanged in everything but name. Still today the people give thanks in the old ways for the
ripening of the corn on a certain saint's day in the high summer and, as
soon as the Sunday Mass in the church is over, the dancing in the village
square begins.

It is perhaps because their material existence is still so close to nature
and because they still have an easy familiarity with it that they have kept

firmly to their beliefs and adapted to cultural pressures without submitting to them. Each of the four Pueblo groups, whether it is the Hopi or Zuni in the west, or the Keresa and Tanoa in the east, knows the mountain ranges where the gods are to be found. They can point out the exact place where the first people emerged from the underground, a place where the crops are also stored in preparation for each new year's abundance. The numerous dancing spirits of rain and fertility, called *kachinas* in the west and *katsina* in the east, participate directly in the many village ceremonies when the men dress up to dance in the elaborate traditional costumes – although again, in the east, this custom is either practised in secret or is disguised as a Christian festival.

This story shows how the mythology of Catholicism has been very lightly grafted on to the old faith. The twelve hidden children of Adam and Eve emerge from the underground world just as long ago the first Pueblo people also emerged. And the story of Jesus is used to show how the Pueblo Indians came to have a nature and a way of life very different from that of the white men and the Mexicans.

Eve had twenty-four children. When they grew up God told her to bring them to be baptized. She was ashamed and hid twelve of them in a cave. So God baptized only twelve of her children.

From the twelve children who were baptized came all the people who are not Indians, the white people. And from the twelve that Eve had hidden in the cave came the Indians.

When God found out that Eve had hidden them in a cave he put them in Mount Blanca in Colorado. It is from there that the Indians came out later, and they then went on to the different pueblos.

When Jesus was born three kings came to visit him and adore him. One was an American, one was a Mexican and the last one was an Indian.

The three kings arrived and knelt down to adore the child. The American gave Jesus money. The Mexican gave Jesus swaddling clothes. The Indian king was very poor and he had nothing to give, so he danced before Jesus.

Jesus told them that he would give them each a gift, and he asked what they wanted. The American said he wanted to be smart and to have power; and Jesus granted him his wish. And that is why the Americans are smart and powerful. The Mexican was asked and he said that he wished to believe in the saints, and to pray, and that is why the Mexicans believe in the saints and pray.

Lastly Jesus asked the Indian king what he wanted. The Indian king said that he was very poor and very humble, and he said that he would accept whatever Jesus offered to him. So Jesus gave him the seeds of corn, wheat and melons, and other fruits. And that is why the Indians have to work all the time in order to stay alive.

THE LAND OF THE DEAD

The gates of the cave
Are shut.
The gates of the cave
Are shut.
The souls of the dead are crowding there in droves.
Like a swarm of flies,
Like a swarm of flies, dancing at evening time[1]

(Les Pygmées de la Fôret Equatoriale by P H Trilles)

THE DEAD ARE A HUGE invisible crowd, a crowd that grows larger with each new generation. They are packed together in a dense mass: under the ground, across the sea, in the air. Sometimes they can be heard as they rush through the spaces of the sky escaping from each other. Sometimes they can be heard fighting together and if one is killed he stands up to fight again. The dead are the unbroken chain which connects time present with the moment when all time began.

The dead watch over the living. They might be protective in their desire to ensure that the continuity of life is not broken; or they might be malicious and determined to trap and kill anyone who does not show them enough respect. Always they are to be feared because they have gone beyond the boundary of death and they cannot be destroyed or controlled by their descendants although they can be manipulated by the appropriate sacrifices and rituals.

The shaman, the medicine-man, the priest: they learn how to listen to the dead, and how to interpret what they are told. If some disaster strikes, it can be that the dead are angry and wish to avenge themselves on the people, and then certain rituals must be performed in order to quieten and appease them. But it can be that a disaster is caused by some other agent, and then the dead stand as witnesses to the suffering of their people. No matter how harsh these watchful ancestors might be in their judgements, they can never desire the extermination of the race, for they themselves would cease to exist if no one was left to speak to them, to feed them or to remember them.

It has often been believed that there will come a day when the dead will return to the land of the living. The moment when that invisible army appears before the eyes of men is the moment when eternity is established on earth. Then the barrier between the two worlds, between the mortal and the immortal, the visible and the invisible, is lifted, and as a result all the limitations of human existence are removed. Everyone from the very old to the very young is reborn into the prime of adult life. And, as it says in the Book of Revelation, 'God shall wipe away all tears from their eyes; and there shall be no more death, neither sorrow nor

crying, neither shall there be any more pain'. [2]

The psychic shock of the arrival of the white men and their demonstration of enormous and seemingly supernatural powers altered the world irrevocably. They might be seen as ancestors or gods or simply as human strangers; they might be treated with fear or respect or hatred. The fact of their existence created a new age. The white men had brought with them a time which had no precedent, a mythical age in which miracles and disasters were to be expected.

The white men had also brought with them countless and hitherto unknown ways of dying. Lethal sicknesses accompanied them and even travelled ahead of them, presaging their arrival. People died of influenza, venereal disease, meningitis, whooping cough and dysentery. They died from changes of diet, from wearing clothes, from drinking alcohol, from fear. They died because they were driven from their land to places where they could not find food or were killed by hostile tribes. They died because they could not grow their crops or because the animals they hunted for food had all been shot. And they died on the battlefields.

Village groups, clans and large tribal communities were confronted with the possibility of genocide. It was no longer the death of individuals which threatened them, but the eradication of the entire race, along with its beliefs, its customs, its past history and its future.

Each newly deceased man, woman and child who joined with the crowd of the invisible dead gave more evidence of the slaughter that was taking place. All the warriors, the chieftains and the wise men were witnesses to what was happening on earth, and either they must save their people or their people would join them in oblivion. The only possibility of salvation lay in the hope that the dead could cross over into the land of the living, drive out the white men and cleanse the world of all its misery so that a new world would come into being:

> He said, 'The Dead will come from the east when the grass is about eight inches high. The deer and the animals will all come back too. The Whites will die out and only the Indians will be left. The Whites will burn up and disappear without even leaving ashes.' (North America) [3]

In order to learn what must be done to prepare for this great event, some people 'died' and went to the land of the dead; others spoke to them in dreams or met them while they walked alone. Very often they were told that the living must first make themselves free from all sin, all anger, and they must have absolute faith in the power of their ancestors:

> The sky will fall on earth and darkness will come. During this darkness all those who did not believe will die. And those who have stolen other people's goods will turn into a snake or a pig. And those who practised sorcery will turn into fishes or into snakes. (Oceania) [4]

LEFT
A battle between Bushmen cattle rustlers and a commando of white farmers is shown in this frieze painted on the rocks at Cold Bokkeveld, north-western cape of South Africa. Around the middle of the nineteenth century this area in East Griqualand was known as 'no-man's land' from which the Bushmen made forays to steal cattle and horses. Their culture was in a process of change similar to that of the North American Indians when they acquired horses from the Spaniards. However the Bushmen were all exterminated before this change could become fully effective.

And so it happened that many disparate groups purified themselves and established new social laws and codes of morality. Tribes accustomed to fighting among each other ceased fighting and those who practised witchcraft gave up their attempts to harm their enemies. The Maoris of New Zealand, the Indians of the Plains of North America, the peoples of Africa and Oceania, numerous warring and unsettled communities united themselves in a concerted attempt to be worthy of the arrival of the new age.

For those who were not warriors there could only be impatient expectation which ultimately led to disillusionment and loss of faith. But for the warriors, the natural fighting people, waiting was in itself a kind of death which they could not endure. For them it was now already time for the great battle with the white men, and soon it would be too late. The dead had to be shown that the living were ready to fight with them. The dead had to be shown how fearlessly the living confronted the white men in order to prove that their present defeat was not due to cowardice, but was caused by a situation which could only be saved by supernatural intervention. Faith makes the impossible come to pass and the living found many ways of proving the strength of their faith. The Xhosas in South Africa destroyed all their food supplies in order to feed the dead who were soon to arrive; the Plains Indians and the Maoris faced the bullets of the white men protected only by their magical prayers and garments.

And when the dead did not rise, then the living often went to join them. In this way the world as it existed for certain peoples, ceased to exist, and perhaps for some this was the only solution open to them.

The Noise

THE MANUS ISLANDERS, Admiralty Islands, Papua New Guinea

Under the political guidance and insight of Paliau (see 'Paliau and Jesus', page 62), the Manus islanders were able to move towards their own modernity but it was a slow process of adaptation and change. A more immediate response came in the form of 'The Noise'. It began on the little island of Rambutjan where a prophet called Wapi predicted that God and the dead ancestors were planning to send quantities of cargo to the island; and in order to prepare themselves and demonstrate their faith the people were told to destroy all their possessions. When the boats and aeroplanes did not arrive, Wapi asked his brothers to murder him because he wanted to go himself to the land of the dead to find out what was happening. However, in spite of Wapi's disillusionment and death, the excitement he had generated was infectious and 'The Noise' spread to other islands.

Each community elaborated its own version of what was soon to happen, usually on the inspiration of someone possessed by a fit of shaking or instructed in a vision. On Manus Island the predictions were given a very practical form when a woman called Piloan went to the nearby island of Tawi and returned with the urgent news that the cargo had already landed there and that she had seen it with her own eyes. And so the people of her village of Peri collected all their property and threw it into the lagoon. Most of the things they threw away belonged to their old society – weapons, tools, sacred objects – and in this way an act of apparently wanton destruction served as a means of severing ties with the past; the dead objects were given to the dead. Some of the American goods were also thrown out in the general enthusiasm. But they were later retrieved from the water and it was said that the sight of the new, valued objects being destroyed shocked people back to their senses and brought an end to 'The Noise'.

All right, when we were on Ndopwa the Noise came to Peri. All right, the people of Peri thought like this, they had heard the talk about The Noise having arrived over at Tawi island, then it took Patusi village and then part of it came to Peri now.

Then the people of Peri heard as follows, 'We must throw away everything inside our houses, throw it all out now. Nothing at all may remain in a house. If there is anything at all left inside a single house, later nothing will appear there. If we throw away everything that is inside our houses completely, all right.

'Then our fathers as well as our grandfathers, some of our brothers also and our mothers, they can bring everything that is ours to come now into our houses to replace all that we have thrown away.

'But whoever does not throw away something that is in his house, when these people, the dead who are coming back to us, when they see that there is something there inside the house, they will not bring everything into the house of this man.'

All right, when they had finished hearing about this, the people went to their houses then. They threw away everything inside the houses – all of the basins, all spears, all canoe paddles, all mats, all good cloth, all of the large bed sheets, along with everything for carpentry and everything used for dressing up. All of this they threw away.

Coquille Jim's Dream

THE PAIUTE INDIANS, Nevada and California, North America

The Dream dance has been going on ever since there has been people in this world. Either a man or a woman dreams something and he has to do it. He has to sing what he dreamed in front of all the people, and they believe in him. One dreamer would die, and another would start in. When you are asleep you dream that you see many people who are dancing and singing. When you wake the next morning you say that you dreamed something good. You tell what the dead people are using – feathers, beads, everything. You remember how they sang.

If the song is good enough the people dance with it for five nights.[5]

Many of the tribes of the Plains and the northwest coast of the United States had always structured aspects of their ritual life around the dreamers who 'died' and then emerged from this trance and returned to the world with songs and revelations for the people. The role played by these visionaries took on a new significance during the latter half of the nineteenth century when the struggle between the Indians and the white men was at its peak. Already the Indians had been heavily defeated both morally and physically and their final doom, although it might be postponed, seemed inevitable. It was from this state of dread and atmosphere of heightened expectation that the Ghost Dance religion emerged.

It first appeared among the Paiutes around the early 1870s and it continued in various forms until the early twentieth century. It spread first among the tribes of California, and later, in the 1890s, among the Plains Indians. The Dance differed widely in its particular mythological structure and significance, but the dancers were all united in their desire to communicate with the inhabitants of the land of the dead and to hasten

and facilitate their return to the land of the living. Many of the tribes already had the belief that this world was bound to grow old and tired. They believed that the day would come when it would finally be destroyed by flames, by a flood, by cracking apart, and then, from out of the chaos a new and rejuvenated world would be born. This idea was suddenly given increased validity by the fact of the white presence. The people were deprived of their land and their freedom to live in the old ways. They saw how the natural world, which had always been treated with great reverence, was being indiscriminately desecrated and so it seemed that the great cataclysm was at hand.

Ghost Dancing was an expression of faith, an expression of the inner conviction that the world which was seen to be dying was sure to be born again. The extremity of the situation united the dancers in their receptivity to commands from the invisible powers. They waited for signs and dreams, for songs and revelations which would teach them to please the gods and the ancestors and to bring the hour of destruction and redemption nearer. They danced for days on end and some said that the rhythmic pounding of their feet on the ground presaged the rumbling of the earth that would soon shake and crack apart. Their ritual dress and activities were seen as reflections of what was already taking place on the invisible plane.

For many of the tribes the Ghost Dance was not anti-white: the white men were simply an aspect of what was seen as a universal psychic disaster. They did say that the white men would be removed by a flood, by a wall of fire, by being swallowed into the ground; they said that the world would be violently purged of all of its troubles and disintegration.

Coquille Jim, whose story is given here, was a leader of one of the early movements which appeared among the Californian Indians in the 1870s. This particular cult was sometimes known as Thompson's Warm House Dance. The account was collected in the 1930s from a Paiute man living on the Siletz Indian Reservation in west Oregon. He is referring back to events which took place when he was still a young child.

Coquille Jim was a big dreamer here at Siletz. He was a fine old man
 with bright eyes that looked right through you. He always dreamed
 of the dead. He said that they would come back but he never said
 when or how – they would just come here all of a sudden. Every
 night he dreamed and in the morning he used to tell what he saw.
 He always had a new song. He was a big dance man too.
One night he saw the dead in a lovely place, the ground was all
 smooth and level like marble. All the people were the same height.
 They were all busy and happy.
One night he dreamed he went to a Dream Dance down here on earth.
 Just as all the people were standing singing with their heads thrown
 back and their arms raised, crying, he saw that the up-above people

were dancing Dream Dances just like those down here, and they were sending their songs to earth.

Then Jim saw a large white house descend from above and stop just about five hundred feet up in the air. Then steps came down from the house, and a person all dressed in red with stars in his hair came

down the steps and invited Coquille Jim to come up. He went right up the stairs and reached the porch of the house. He heard singing inside. He heard a big noise. He sat down in a fine chair. It was a glass house. A white man sat there with white hair and a white beard.

The white man asked Jim if he saw people. He told him that eyes, hands, fingers to get food, all these things had been made to give the Indians an easy life so that they wouldn't have to dig and plant in order to live. All the wild things had been provided for the Indians.

Then the white man turned and seemed to open a window. Jim saw the Modoc War with all the dead whites. The man showed him in another direction where there were a million million people.

Wovoka's Message

THE PAIUTE INDIANS, Nevada and California, North America

> When the sun died I went up to heaven and I saw God and all the people who had died a long time ago. God told me to come back and tell my people they must be good and love one another and not fight or steal or lie. He gave me this dance to give to my people.[6]

Wovoka was a Paiute Indian from the desert Plains of Nevada. He was the instigator of the second Ghost Dance movement which spread eastwards from California during the late nineteenth century, eventually effecting more than 30 Indian tribes.

Wovoka's father had been a leading figure in the Ghost Dancing of the 1870s and essentially his message was the same as the one preached by his visionary predecessors. He said that the dead would rise and return to the land of the living, bringing with them a new age of peace and plenty; and to hasten this moment the people must dance and sing according to a new sacred ceremony. He also instructed them to prepare themselves morally, so that they might be worthy of participating in the eternal happiness of a world reborn. His message was a simple one but it made exacting demands on the people. Remarkably, he wanted them to tolerate the presence of the white men and he asked them to love each other and to 'do right always'. In saying that they must no longer weep for their dead he was forbidding the customary demonstrations of grief when people would kill their horses, burn their possessions and lacerate their bodies when confronted by death. Such a practice had become far more devastating in its effects now that so many unknown epidemics were sweeping among the tribes. He also forbade fighting. In so doing he was demanding that the traditional warrior spirit of such tribes as the Ute, the Cheyenne and the Pawnee be held in check, and it was a proof of his power that these tribes did cease in their hostilities towards each other.

Wovoka himself had been partially adopted by a white farmer who

129

had given him the name of Jack Wilson and perhaps this explains his conciliatory attitude to the white men. Although the white men were to have no place in his vision of the new world, he did not wish for the people or for supernatural agencies to destroy the intruders; they were simply to be removed from Indian territory and returned to their own land.

It was in 1889, during a total eclipse of the sun and while he was lying sick with a fever, that Wovoka had his first vision of heaven and was instructed by God how he must lead the people. He was given his message; he was told how the Dance must be performed and he was also given 'five songs for naming rain, the first of which brings on a mist or cloud, the second a snowfall, the third a shower, and the fourth a hard rain or storm, while when he sings the fifth song the weather again becomes clear'.[7]

The eastern tribes of the North American Plains had an urgent need for a prophet and leader to give them hope again. Wovoka's fame spread with great rapidity and soon he was receiving numerous delegations who came to him for advice and instruction. He attempted to maintain the continuity of his teachings, instructing the people in the dances and the songs, providing them with red ochre paint to decorate their bodies and giving them written copies of his message of salvation. But inevitably his words were altered by the temperament of his listeners and the various situations of the tribes. Inadvertently he set a huge movement into motion and he himself was horrified by the part he was said to have played and even tried to forbid the dancing from going on. When the battlefield disaster of Wounded Knee took place in 1890 in what is now South Dakota, he was held by some to be directly responsible.

It was under the auspices of the United States Government at Washington that the ethnographer James Mooney was sent to study the Ghost Dance. Between 1890 and 1893 he lived and worked among the Indians of the Plains. Thanks to his close contact with them and his deep sympathy for them in their predicament he made an extraordinary study of the fascinating Ghost Dance religion. In 1892 he went to visit Wovoka, acting as the representative for certain Cheyenne and Arapaho friends. The meeting was a success and when Mooney returned to them in Oklahoma these friends demonstrated their increased trust and confidence in him by revealing their most secret information concerning the Ghost Dance. They showed him the two copies of Wovoka's message which were in their possession, and it is Mooney's translation of these which is given here.

When you get home you must make a dance to continue five days. Dance four successive nights, and the last night keep up the dance until the morning of the fifth day, when all must bathe in the river and then disperse to their homes. You must all do in the same way. I, Jack Wilson, love you all, and my heart is full of gladness for the

A Ghost Dance dress of painted buckskin is decorated with the bright images from a dream vision. It belonged to an Indian woman of the Arapaho tribe and she is probably the central figure standing under a crescent moon. The flying birds are symbols of transcendence, while the turtle represents material existence.

gifts you have brought me. When you get home I shall give you a
good rain cloud which will make you feel good. I give you a good
spirit and give you all good paint. I want you to come again in three
months, some from each tribe there on the Indian Territory.
There will be a good deal of snow this year and some rain. In the fall
there will be such a rain as I have never given you before.
Grandfather the Messiah says, when your friends die you must not
cry. You must not hurt anybody or do harm to anyone. You must
not fight. Do right always. It will give you satisfaction in life.
Do not tell the white people about this. Jesus is now upon the earth.
He appears like a cloud. The dead are all alive again. I do not know
when they will be here; maybe this fall or in the spring. When the
time comes there will be no more sickness and everyone will be
young again.
Do not refuse to work for the whites and do not make any trouble
with them until you leave them. When the earth shakes at the coming
of the new world do not be afraid. It will not hurt you.
I want you to dance every six weeks. Make a feast at the dance and
have food that everybody may eat. Then bathe in the water. That is
all. You will receive good words again from me some time. Do not
tell lies.

Short Bull

THE SIOUX INDIANS, South Dakota and Nebraska, North America

When I was a boy the Sioux owned the world; the sun rose and set
on their land; they sent ten thousand men to battle. Where are the
warriors today? Who slew them? Where are our lands? Who owns
them?[8]

For the Sioux the Ghost Dance took on a new meaning. Between the
1860s and the 1880s they had suddenly been deprived of everything that
they knew as their own. Accustomed to the freedom of the Plains, the
encroachment of the white men meant that they were now restricted to
reservations; the right to perform their sacred Sun Dance ceremony was
denied to them and the herds of buffalo had been exterminated within a
period of eight years. The little land left to the Sioux was arid and useless
and they were made dependent on government rations to keep them from
starving. They said that the Great Spirit had sent the white man to them
to punish them for their sins, but this punishment could not be indefinite
and soon the Great Spirit would show mercy and remove their persecutors.

In 1889 a delegation went to Nevada to meet Wovoka the prophet and
to learn more about the coming millennium. A few months after the
return of this expedition the Ghost Dance had been adopted by the
majority of the Sioux. Again, there was the belief in the return of the dead

and the rebirth of the world, but the predictions took on a more violent form. There would be landslides, floods, storms and whirlwinds; and there would also be great battles between the two races when the Great Spirit would protect the Sioux and make them invulnerable to the bullets which were fired at them. Then when the chaos had passed and all the white men lay dead, the Indians would again be owners of the infinite stretches of the Plains and the buffalo and the wild game would again be seen moving across the landscape in their countless numbers.

A Sioux by the name of Short Bull was one of those who visited Wovoka and on his return he became a leader of the Dance. This sermon was delivered by him on 31 October 1890 at the Pine Ridge Reservation in South Dakota. The ethnographer James Mooney was present at the occasion.

Short Bull describes what will happen on the last day. The tree he refers to is the sacred pole that was always erected at the centre of a dance circle. He says that when all the people gather at Pass Creek on that day when the world will end, they must strip themselves naked as a sign of their willingness to let go of the present time and allow a new time to come into being.

My friends and relations, I Short Bull, will soon start this thing in running order. I have told you that it would come to pass in two seasons that the dead Indian nation would come home, but now, since the whites are interfering so much I will advance the time from what my father told me. The time will be shorter. Therefore you must not be afraid of anything. Some of my relations have no ears, I will have them blown away.

A tree will sprout up, and there all the members of our religion and our tribe must gather together. That will be the place where we will see our dead relations.

Before this time we must dance the balance of this moon. Then the earth will shiver very hard. When this thing occurs I will start the wind to blow. We are the ones who will see our fathers, mothers and everybody. We, the tribe of Indians are the ones who are living the sacred life. God, our father himself, has told and commanded and shown me to do these things.

Our father in heaven has placed a mark at each point of the four winds. First he has placed a clay pipe which lies at the setting of the sun and represents the Sioux tribe. Second, there is a holy arrow lying at the north which represents the Cheyenne tribe. Third, at the rising of the sun there lies hail, which represents the Arapaho tribe. Fourth, there lies a pipe and a nice feather in the south, and this represents the Crow tribe. My father has shown me these things and therefore we must continue this dance.

If the soldiers surround you four deep, then three of you on whom I have put holy shirts will sing a song, which I have taught you. And

when you sing this song around the soldiers, some of them will drop
dead. Then the rest of them will start to run, but their horses will
sink into the earth. Then you can do as you desire with them.

Now, you must know this, that all the soldiers and that white race
will be dead. There will be only five thousand of them left living on
the earth. My friends and relations, this is straight and true.

Now we must gather at Pass Creek where the tree is sprouting. There
we will go among our dead relatives. You must not take any earthly
things with you. The men must take off all their clothing and the
women must do the same. No one shall be ashamed of exposing their
bodies. My father has told us to do this and we must do as he says.

You must not be afraid of anything. The guns are the only things we
are afraid of, but the guns belong to our father in heaven and he will
see that they do us no harm. Whatever the white men may tell you,
do not listen to them. This is all.

The Rituals of the Ghost Dance

THE OGLALA SIOUX INDIANS, South Dakota and Nebraska, North America

Verily I have given you my strength,
Says the father, says the father.
The shirt will cause you to live,
Says the father, says the father.[9]

This is an account of a second visit made by delegates from the Sioux
tribe to Wovoka in 1890. It was originally written down by an Oglala
Sioux named George Sword and it appears in James Mooney's study of
the Ghost Dance.

Wovoka could inspire people with his words and he was able to
make them 'see' the spirit world he was speaking of. One Arapaho Indian
told how he had watched him wave eagle feathers over his hat, and then,
when he withdrew his hand, he 'saw the whole world'. On the occasion
of this gathering Wovoka is reported to have evoked a similar vision for
those present.

Wovoka felt himself to have been chosen by God as a leader and a
prophet. From his connection with the Wilson family he had adopted a
number of Christian images and tenets but he never identified himself
with Christ, claimed that he was marked with the stigmata or that he had
supernatural powers greater than those of other healers and medicine-
men. It was the people who came to him who gave him the attributes of
a semi-divine being, saying that he was Christ the King who had been
persecuted and crucified by the white men and who had now returned to
earth as an Indian. George Sword's account is an example of this kind
of exaggeration.

At this meeting Wovoka instructed the people how they must paint
their bodies and decorate their holy ghost shirts. Most tribes wore their

finest shirts and dresses of buckskin for the Dance and it was only among the Sioux that white shirts were worn and considered to have the magical properties of a protective armour. Again, this is something for which Wovoka disclaimed all responsibility.

Ghost shirts and dresses were often worn by the dancing men, women and children. They were decorated with symbols taken from Indian mythology as well as from aspects of the white man's culture. The images used were often based on the visions experienced by someone who had 'died' and seen what the people in the land of the dead were wearing.

The people said that the messiah will come at a place in the woods where the place was prepared for him. When we went to the place a smoke descended from heaven to the place where he was to come. When the smoke disappeared, there was a man of about forty, which was the Son of God. The man said:

'My grandchildren! I am glad you have come far away to see your relatives. These are your people who have come back from your country.' When he said he wanted us to go with him, we looked and we saw a land which was created and which reached across the ocean. It disappeared, he saying that it was not the time for that to take place.

The messiah then gave to Good Thunder some paints – Indian paints and a white paint – and green sagebrush twigs. He said, 'My grandchildren, on your way home, if you kill any buffalo cut the head, the tail, and the four feet and leave them, and that buffalo will come to live again. When the soldiers of the white people chief want to arrest me, I shall stretch out my arms, which will knock them into nothingness, or, if not that, the earth will open and swallow them in.

'My father commanded me to visit the Indians on a purpose. I went to the white people first, but they not good. They killed me, and you can see the marks of my wounds on my feet, my hands, and on my back. My father has given you life – your old life – and you have come to see your friends. But you will not take me home with you at this time. I want you to tell your people when you get home to follow my examples. Any one Indian who does not obey me and tries to be on white's side will be covered over by a new land that is to come over this old one. You will, all the people, use the paints and the sagebrush twigs I give you. In the spring when the green grass comes, your people who have gone before you will come back again. You shall see your friends then, for you have come to my call.'

In the following spring the people began to gather at the White Clay Creek. Just at this time Kicking Bear went on a visit to the Arapaho tribe, and said that the Arapaho there have ghost dancing. He said that people dancing would get crazy and die, and that then the messiah is seen and all the ghosts. When they die they see strange things, they see their relatives who died long before. The person

dancing becomes dizzy and finally drops dead, and the first thing
they saw is an eagle come to them and carried them to where the
messiah is with his ghosts.

The persons in the ghost dancing are all joined hands. A man stands
and then a woman, so in this way forming a very large circle. They
dance around in the circle in a continuous time until some of them
become so tired and overtired that they become crazy and finally
drop as though dead, with foam in mouth all wet with sweat.

All the men and women made holy shirts and dresses they wear in
dance. The persons dropped in the dance would all lie in the great
dust the dancing made. They paint white muslin, they make holy
shirts and dresses out of it with blue across the back, and alongside
this a line of yellow paint. They also paint in the front part of the
shirts and dresses. A picture of an eagle is made on the back. On the
shoulders and on the sleeves they tied eagle feathers. They say that
the bullets will not go through these shirts and dresses, so they all
have these dresses for war. Their enemies' weapons will not go
through these dresses.

The ghost dancers wear an eagle feather on their head, and any man is

LEFT
The Ghost Dance of the Cheyenne and Arapaho Indians is shown in this pictograph drawn in coloured inks on buckskin. It was made by an Ute Indian called Yellow Nose who was a captive of the Cheyenne in 1891. A ring of dancers surround the isolated central figures, some of whom are carrying sacred objects while others wave pieces of cloth to hasten the arrival of a trance state.

RIGHT
The sacred wheel was an important symbol to the Sioux Indians as it represented the universe to which all people belonged. One of the rituals of the Ghost Dance involved hanging a wheel, a bow and other items onto a Ghost Dance tree. In this detail, a dancer is shown holding a wheel and sacred sticks.

made crazy if he is fanned with this feather. In the ghost dance no person is allowed to wear anything made of any metal, except that guns made of metal are carried by some of the dancers.

When they came from the ghosts they brought meat with them. They also brought water, fire and wind with which to kill all the whites, or Indians who will help the chief of the whites. They made sweat houses and made holes in the middle of the sweat houses where they say that the water will come out. Before they begin to dance they all raise their hands towards the northwest and cry in supplication to the messiah and then they begin the dance with the song:

> The whole world is coming,
> A nation is coming, a nation is coming,
> The Eagle has brought the message to the tribe.
> The father says so, the father says so.
> Over the whole earth they are coming.
> The buffalo are coming, the buffalo are coming,
> The Crow has brought the message to the tribe,
> The father says so, the father says so. [10]

The Starvation of the Xhosas

THE XHOSAS, South Africa

The Xhosas were one of the most warlike and powerful tribes of South Africa. Between the spring of 1856 and the spring of 1857 more than three-quarters of them died of self-inflicted starvation. The only figures available are from what was then British-owned Xhosa land. There the numbers dropped from 105,000 to 37,000 and this was estimated to be less of a drop in Xhosa numbers than in other areas. This is the story of what happened.

A young girl went down to the river to fetch water and there she met a group of strangers whose appearance was different from the appearance of other people. She told her uncle and he went and saw them and spoke with them. He recognized one of them as his brother, a man who had died in battle several years previously. The strangers said that they were the dead warriors who had come from battlefields across the sea to help the Xhosas drive out the English. They said that if the people followed their instructions all the long-dead ancestors would rise and join forces with the living. But to make this happen certain things must be done.

The most powerful chief of the Xhosas, a man named Kreli, heard of the arrival of the dead and rejoiced at the possibility of defeating the English. He obeyed the instructions enthusiastically and all the lesser chiefs followed his example.

At first the strangers simply said that the best cattle must be killed and eaten, but then the need for slaughter gathered momentum and more and more animals needed to be killed in order to feed the dead. Not only did the dead want blood, they wanted grain as well and bit by bit all the fields were burnt to the ground and all the grain reserves were destroyed.

In the early months of 1857 the people were starving and wild with anticipation for they had nothing more to give. Not only were the dead expected, but also the cattle would return fatter than ever and the granaries would again be filled. In preparation large compounds were erected for the animals and enormous skin bags were stitched to hold the fresh milk.

A day was chosen as the appointed last day, and then when nothing happened the people lost hope. The girl who had first met the strangers managed to survive. Later the British Government organized a public inquiry into the recent events and this account is taken from the girl's testimony.

The beginning of all the trouble was a message sent by Kreli to Mhala. The message was, 'Kill all your cattle, Mhala; we will go and fight for the English cattle'.

My name is Nongqause. Mhala was my uncle, I lived with him on the Gxara River near the sea coast. Mhala is dead. He died about six moons ago (October 1857). The cause of his death was starvation during the famine. Mhala had many cattle before the talk about the

new people began. It was then that I told him how I had seen ten
strange men in the garden, and that I was afraid to go there.

The people I saw were 'Kafirs'[11] and they were young men, and I did
not know them and I was afraid of them. Mhala said they would not
harm me, and he told me to speak to them and ask them what they
were doing there in the garden.

I asked them, and they said, 'We are the people who have come to
order you to kill your cattle, to burn your corn and to stop all work'.

And when they were asked what we would then have left to eat they
said, 'We will find you something to eat'.

They came again and I asked them who had sent them and they said,
'We have come of our own accord. We wish for everything in this
country to be made new, and we have come from a place of refuge.'

And so it was that on the next day my uncle Mhala killed one head of
cattle, and he called a meeting of the people and told them how the
strangers had come to tell them to kill their cattle and destroy their
corn, saying that plenty more would be provided for them
afterwards. Then the people went off and from that day they began
the killing. Mhala killed one animal each day. The people killed more
cattle than they could use and the dogs and the wild beasts ate many
of the carcasses.

About four days later we saw the ten men in the garden, Mhala took
me with him to speak to them, and I asked them for news. They
said, 'We do not know what news you expect from us. All that we
have to say is that you must kill your cattle and destroy your corn.'

Five days later only two of the men came, and they said, 'Our Great
Chief has sent us to tell you that all the people must kill all the cattle.
He wishes to change this country. He wants you to tell this to all the
chiefs.'

I asked them who their great chief was, but they would not name him
as we had not met him, or heard of him and we would not know
him.

My uncle Mhala went to the chief who is between the Kei and the
Bashee Rivers and told him the news. And he visited other kraals so
that the news was spread all over the country.

Three strangers appeared in the garden and I heard them say to
Mhala, 'You must be quick in killing your cattle, in seven days the
people will rise'.

I asked the men 'What people?' and they said, 'The same people as
ourselves, the dead ancestors of the Xhosa people who are going to
return. They will rise at different kraals with cattle, corn, guns, and
assegais,[12] and they will drive the English out of the country, and
make them run into the sea.'

Within seven days Mhala had killed all his cattle, and all the people
had killed their cattle. After the seven days had passed the people
waited for the return of the ancestors. They waited for two red suns

ABOVE
*Rifles and guns are often
represented as images of power and
prestige in art, as with this
ornamental head-rest made by the
Mashona people of Rhodesia in the
last century.*

to rise over the hills in the east. Then the heavens would fall on the English and crush them. But the sun rose and set as usual and the ancestors did not come.
My uncle stayed in that place for ten days and then he went down towards the sea where he could try to live on roots and shellfish. And when we were starving I often heard him say that he regretted killing the cattle, and destroying his corn.

The Hau-hau Movement

THE MAORIS, New Zealand

> Friends, this is a word from God to you: if any minister or other European comes to this place, do not protect him; he must die, die, die.[13]

In 1840 the British Governor of New Zealand drew up the Treaty of Waitangi which gave to the British Crown the sole right to buy up Maori land. The buying rate was six pennies an acre and the Crown then sold its newly acquired property to settlers for one pound an acre.

After an initial wariness the Maoris had welcomed the white men and Christianity. Their first encounters with the missionaries were in 1814 and by 1840 it was said that half of the Maori population had been willingly converted. It was considered good for prestige to 'adopt' a white man into a village community and the Maori chiefs readily sold off portions of their territory. Later they were to say, 'The missionaries turned our eyes to heaven, and then turned their eyes to the land'.

When the early feelings of disquiet were felt, the Maoris had attempted to take practical action. They formed land leagues to check the loss of property and in 1857 one large group of tribes held an important general meeting where they elected a king. They declared that they were willing to maintain their love and allegiance to the British Queen and the Governor, but they wanted to have their own judicial system and government as well. Their system of kingship was modelled on that of the Old Testament and in electing a Maori king they resolved to put an end to the long tradition of bloody tribal wars and ceaseless pursuits of revenge which had divided the Maoris among themselves for so long.

In spite of these initiatives, by 1860 the Maoris had 'had to convince themselves that the colonial administration, now lined up against them, was backing the unjust demands of the white farmers with its guns and was determined to have its way or destroy the native population. In the face of this unexpected realization, the Maori developed a mortal hate of the British, and took up arms to defend their rights!' [14]

The Maori Wars lasted from 1863 to 1865. Many innocent tribespeople were killed or dispossessed and large areas of land were confiscated by the government. It was from this state of desolation that the Hau-hau movement was born. A factor behind the speed of the movement's growth was the consent given by the authorities to the mutilation of a great Maori chief's corpse so that a British doctor could preserve a piece of his tatooed skin.

The leader of the Hau-hau movement was a man called Te Ua. He had been a Maori priest and later a Wesleyan convert. First he had prophesied that an English ship would be wrecked off the Taranaki coast, and it was. Then he predicted that if he and his followers were to attack a certain English regiment they would be victorious, and they were. After this battle the Maoris drank the blood of the dead English soldiers and acquired the decapitated head of the regiment's leader, Captain Lloyd. The head was cured and held aloft on a pole as a symbol of the movement and the means by which the Angel Gabriel was able to communicate directly with his prophet Te Ua.

Gabriel told Te Ua to erect poles with long ropes attached to them to enable the angels of the wind (the word *hau* literally means wind and also life-energy) to descend to earth and help chase out the white people. The ceremonies were performed by men, women and children, all naked; and they would build up into a frenzy of prophecy and possession as the people marched round and round the pole chanting songs based partly on military orders, partly on church hymns and partly on incomprehensible sounds.

The Hau-hau followers believed that the magical intervention of Gabriel and the Virgin Mary would make them invulnerable to the bullets of the white men. There were a few disastrous confrontations between unarmed chanting Maori and what amounted to a firing squad. The movement was brought to a halt in 1866; Te Ua was arrested and subsequently released, and many of his supporters were deported.

The Maoris drank the blood of the dead English soldiers and cut off their heads, burying them in separate places to their bodies. A few days later the Angel Gabriel appeared to these men who had drunk the blood. He told them that they must dig up Captain Lloyd's head and cure it in the way that was the custom among them. Then they must parade the head all over New Zealand. The Angel Gabriel said that from this time onwards the head would be the medium of communication between the Maori people and Jehovah.

The head was dug up. It spoke and declared that the man Te Ua was

to be the high priest of the movement, and Hepaniah and Rangitauira were to be his assistants. It told them that this new religion was to be called *Pai Marire* which means the good and the beautiful.

The head promised that the Angel Gabriel and his legions of helpers would protect them from their enemies the white men. It said that the Virgin Mary would always be with them. It said that the religion of England as it was taught in the scripture books was false, and the scripture books must all be burnt.

The head declared that every day of the week was a sacred day, and no notice should be taken of the Christian sabbath. Men and women must all live together and sleep together, so that the children of the Maoris would be as numerous as the sands on the sea shore.

The priests of the Pai Marire had superhuman powers; they could obtain victory for their followers by shouting out the word 'Hau!' The people who believed in the religion would soon drive all the whites out of New Zealand. This was to happen as soon as the head of Captain Lloyd had been carried to all parts of the island. Legions of angels were standing by waiting for the commands of the priests, and when the time came they were to help the Maoris exterminate the whites.

And it would happen that when the last white man had perished in the sea, then all the Maoris who had died since the beginning of the world would leap up from their graves with a shout and stand in the presence of Te Ua, the Great Prophet. The deaf would hear, the blind see, the lame walk. Every disease would disappear and all would be perfect in their bodies and in their spirits. Men would be sent down from heaven to teach the Maoris all the arts and sciences known by the white men.

The priests had the power to teach the Maoris the English language in just one lesson, but that could only happen provided that all the people assembled at a certain time in a certain place before a tall flagstaff bearing a flag of a certain colour.

There was one old Maori woman who had bought some clothes in the town of Wanganui, and these were wrapped up in newspaper. Te Ua's assistant Rangitauira obtained this paper, and read what was written there to a crowd of people who all believed that he was speaking to them in English. He said that the newspaper contained a report of the Waitorara War in which three thousand white soldiers had been killed along with four hundred Maoris who had been friendly to them.

And it was also written in that newspaper that the Queen of England wished it to be made known that when this war was over then all the surviving Maoris who had been friendly to the English would be taken to Europe where they would be used as beasts of burden by the white men. They would be made to sweep his streets, and clean up the most filthy places in his cities.

LEFT
Te Ua, the leader of the Hau-hau movement in New Zealand.

145

The Goddess Djēwmé

THE MAMBERAMO, West Papua New Guinea

Djēwmé will come with the warria and bring cargo for us;
When they come out of the graves they will give it to us.
We hear the sound of the surf already rising from the graves.
We hear the sound of the surf;
The warria are bringing cargo and putting it on the graves. [15]

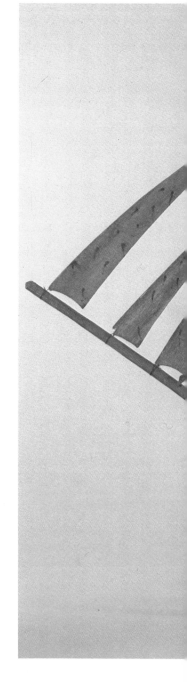

Above the earth lies the village of the dead. The spirits who live there are called the *warria*. They are rich and happy and always have a plentiful supply of pigs, sago, breadfruit and tobacco. The women shed their skins like snakes so they never appear old. People can dance for night after night without getting tired.

A man dies. His corpse is placed on a raised platform and left to decompose. The people of the Mamberamo area of Papua New Guinea believe that the goddess Djēwmé and a group of warria then come to fetch his spirit and lead it to the village of the dead. On the way they stop in the tall tree that is Djēwmé's home. When the body of the dead man on the platform has become clean bones his spirit is free to leave the tree and go to the village. If in his life he has been powerful – a story teller, the father of many children, a skilled hunter – then he will become a warria. The same applies to a woman who has worked hard, or a child who has been remarkable in some way.

At the time of the 'burial of the bones' a huge feast is prepared and guests from all around are invited. The women go to the sago swamps and prepare as much food as they can. The men kill wild pigs and domestic pigs, birds and fish, iguanas and cassowaries and other creatures. This is the occasion on which the living can make contact with the dead. They offer gifts of food to Djēwmé and the warria, and to the new dead man who has just joined them. In return they hope that they will not be allowed to go hungry.

The people in this area of New Guinea have always had to struggle for their existence. The women grow bananas and papayas in their small gardens and gather sago in the swamps. The men go hunting. But often the food shortage is so severe that they must live on larvae and leaves gathered in the forest. As a result, religious activity is always centred around the production of food. The women do the practical work of gathering it, the men do the ritual work of ensuring that more can be obtained. They say, 'The women can only work what we create'. [16]

In contrast to the harsh life of the living there is the state of eternal opulence enjoyed by the dead. They say that once this paradise was with the people on earth; but then they insulted Djēwmé and she removed herself, her people and her plenty from them. They also say that one day she means to return. Sometimes a few of the warria come to a village bringing perhaps a gift of pigs with them and giving advice and reassurance. They do not appear as fearful ghosts, but as familiar figures,

'The men wear the stomach shield and headdress just as we do. And they all speak our language.'[17]

The arrival of the white men and their goods created a new picture of the village of the dead and the good things it contained. It was not just the shortage of pigs and sago that the people now felt, but the shortage of cargo as well. The fact that the white men were able to acquire their goods without working gave validity to the old myth and made the people impatient for the arrival of their long-awaited time of plenty. It became apparent that Djēwmé and the warria were not able to arrive while the white men remained in the area.

This text is based on an event which took place between 1955 and 1956 when the death of a little child sparked off a new set of rituals and Djēwmé and the warria appeared to the people explaining how they would soon come to settle in the area, bringing with them eternal life, eternal happiness and quantities of cargo.

A long time ago, in the very beginning, Djēwmé came to this place and brought her pigs with her. Before that time the people here knew only the cassowary. No one knows where Djēwmé came from. She is a very tall woman. Her skin is light in colour, though not as completely white as the skin of Europeans. She has long fair hair.

When Djēwmé first came to the Mamberamo area she built a village for the dead, a very big village. Since that time all of our dead and also the dead of the other tribes east of the Mamberamo go to that village.

When Djēwmé had supplied the village of the dead with sago and many many pigs she also brought pigs and other animals to living men. They immediately began shooting them and giving big feasts. They invited people from far and near to join in the eating, dancing and singing. All these people were in a very good humour because of the pigs and the other animals. But they made one big mistake. Djēwmé had warned them not to dance and sing and laugh in the day-time because they were eating her pigs. But the people did not listen, and they danced and sang while the bright sun was shining.

And so Djēwmé left the land of the living and went to the village of the dead where the sun does not shine. But she did not disappear for ever. One day she promised she would return with the spirits of the dead, the warria, and then the people here would have the same abundance of food and the same riches as are now found in the village of the dead. Never again would anybody fall ill, never again would anyone die, and the dead would come out of their graves.

And then it happened, not so long ago (about 1955–56), that a little child died in the village of Kwatani. In order to find out who had killed the child, the father and the uncle went to catch a fish in the Mamberamo river. They immediately caught one and it struck them as being an unusual kind. They cut a small piece from the fish, mixed it with parts of the flesh of the dead boy, and threw the fish, still alive, back into the river. Then the boy's father and uncle ate part of this mixture and the uncle kept the rest.

That very night, while the boy's corpse was still resting on the scaffold on which the bodies of the dead are placed until they have decomposed, Djēwmé and a large group of the warria came to see the father and the uncle. They told the uncle to cut down the scaffold and bury the corpse before it was fully decomposed. They said that the two of them must build a good house over the grave, and that the people of the village were to plant flowers all around it.

The people of the village did as they were told. They built a good house over the grave and planted a double row of flowers. When night came they all assembled at the new house over the boy's grave. No one was missing.

That same night Djēwmé and the warria appeared again. Djēwmé came first in order to open up the way for the warria. This time the warria, both male and female, and Djēwmé herself, were dressed in white clothes like Europeans. In spite of this the people recognized them immediately. They shook hands with them and said, 'Welcome back to our village'. Then they started singing and dancing, to give full honour to their new lords and masters. Beating their drums they sang:

Our drums, our drums,
Hear the sound of our drums over the grave.

After this song of welcome, Djēwmé and the warria told the people that they would soon come back again to stay with them for ever. 'But first,' they said, 'go and tell the other tribes to make preparations to meet us; as soon as all the people know of our coming we will return again with ships full of clothing, axes, tobacco, machetes, outboard motors, and other cargo.'

A sure sign of their return will be the sound of the sea coming into the graves. 'When you hear the sound of the surf coming up from the graves,' Djēwmé told the people, 'then the ships will be near.' The sea, carrying the ships, will come into the graves. Then the dead will rise and board the ships. Then the ships will become visible to the living. All the ships will be loaded with cargo, well packed in cases and trunks. The warria will unload these cases and trunks and store them above the graves. Then nobody will lack anything. There will be a new village. Nobody will fall ill any more, no one will die, and all the tribes of the Mamberamo area will be as rich as Europeans.

THE AFTERMATH

*Indians ain't got nothing from God. But you white people you got
everything; you got that book the Bible, you got power. But the
Indians got nothing. In a little while, towards the end, God give us
peyote. That's how we happen to find God.*[1]
(Menomini Peyotism by J S Slotkin)

THE AFTERMATH comes when all the beliefs and traditions of the past are no longer valid, and the people find themselves alienated from their own history. It comes when they can no longer believe that soon, next year when the grass is knee-high, next year when a great wind begins to blow, they will be saved from their despair. Suddenly the age of miracles has come to an end and the people cannot maintain the hope that the accumulated power of their watching gods or their dead ancestors will rise up to defeat the white strangers, intruders and conquerors. Then it is necessary to confront the reality of the present time, and to learn to survive within it, both physically and spiritually.

At first it was the white men who were the strangers in a land which did not belong to them and which they did not understand, but in the time of the aftermath it is the people who find that they have been turned into aliens, living in a country which is not theirs by right and controlled by laws and taboos which seem meaningless and unjust. Black Elk told of an Indian holy man called Drinks Water who prophesied that a strange race was going to weave a spider's web around the people, saying, 'When this happens you shall live in square grey houses in a barren land, and beside those square grey houses you shall starve'.[2] In the time of the aftermath those who had managed to survive the diseases, the battles and the other lethal consequences of this new age, must now learn a different sort of survival if they are to save themselves from spiritual annihilation.

This last section tells of a few of the prophets, leaders and mythological heroes who were able to provide the people with certain rituals and beliefs which helped them to make the transition into a changed world. It also reveals a little about how this world appeared to some people, and what they needed to forget and learn in order to be able to live in it. There were those who made use of aspects of the white man's culture, turning its mystery into their own, while others violently rejected everything that their oppressors had imported, maintaining a state of angry separatism. There were also those whose response took the form of a spiritual detachment from all outside pressures and threats; people like the members of the peyote cult which was adopted by many of the North American Indian tribes, who learnt to live with their sadness without animosity, declaring, 'I feel pity for everyone'.

Abel went on a magical journey to heaven and he found it to be a place

RIGHT
*An image of Christ on the cross as
portrayed by an artist from Papua
New Guinea. This piece, which
was produced after the Second
World War, shows the influence of
mission examples combined with a
traditional art style.*

inhabited by jaguars and other creatures from the South American jungle, as well as by dancing archangels. He said that if the people did not follow him and persisted in trusting in the official Christian religion, then they would always be the servants of the white men. Kelevi believed in God and Jesus Christ, but he accused the Methodist minister of being an incarnation of the old Fijian snake god Degei, the one whom the missionaries called Satan. Johnny-The-Thunderer-Comes-With-Noise-Of-Thunder, a leader of the North American Indian Drum Religion, visited the land of the dead in a dream vision, and he saw that a white man with a stick in his hand stood guard at the foot of the stairs leading to heaven, and he beat any Indian who approached this place which did not belong to them and which they would never be allowed to enter.

Perhaps it is the story of Tail Feather Woman which tells most vividly what can be meant by the aftermath. They say that there was a battle between the white soldiers and the Sioux Indians, and on the Indian side everyone was killed except for one woman. She escaped by lying submerged in water hidden by reeds, and she remained there for several days until a man who was a god came to her and pitied her. He led her to the camp of the white soldiers, and she sat down amongst them and ate their food but they could not see her and she came to no harm. Tail Feather Woman was then instructed in the rituals of the Drum Religion, or Powwow as it came to be called, and she taught it to the Comanche tribe and they taught it to others. It was a religion for people who had almost lost their hope and their will to live, and it enabled them to maintain their dignity and identity as an independent race in spite of their predicament of defeat and isolation.

But the selection of texts included here is not a conclusion to the theme of this book. The aftermath is not an indefinite state but a state of transition, and the meetings between the white men and the people who had no previous knowledge of their existence belongs to such recent history that there is still no perspective of distance with which to judge the implications of all that has been happening.

Battiste Good's Vision

THE DAKOTA SIOUX INDIANS, South Dakota and Nebraska, North America

During the nineteenth century the Dakotas kept calender records of their past history in the form of pictographic charts drawn on buffalo hides, cloth or even paper. These were called the 'counting backs' or winter counts, the word winter referring to the year as a whole as well as to the cold season. Each year was represented by an image of some significant event by which it could be remembered: 'brought-home-horse-with-his-tail-braided-with-eagle-feathers-winter', 'measles-and-sickness-used-up-the-people-winter', 'star-passed-by-with-loud-noise-winter'. Because the counts were used by all the many bands of Dakota, they differed in their choice of what was considered significant in a

Fig. 1.

particular year. But they all share a concern with such major events as the spread of a famine or an epidemic.

Battiste Good's winter count is different from the others in that it is not simply concerned with the recent factual past. It opens with a painting of a hill, a bird, two blue arcs and two American flags, and this is the vision which Battiste received in the year 1856 when Eagle Woman came to him and told him of the past heritage and the future destiny of the Dakotas. Then follow 13 figures which trace the mythological origins of the Dakotas from the year 900 when The-Woman-From-Heaven came to them to the year 1700 when the people hunted the buffalo using the only horse they possessed. From 1700 to 1880 his count follows the orthodox pattern, giving a separate image for each year and ending with 'sent-the-boys-and-girls-to-school-winter'. It is said that Battiste was able to go so far back in time by asking the very old people what names they remembered for the years and he then arranged them chronologically.

In 1880 Battiste gave a copy of his completed winter count to a certain Reverend Cleveland and he also explained to him the meaning of his vision, his mythology and his record of Dakota history. At the time when Eagle Woman came flying over his head in the sacred Black Hills, the first Land Agreements were being drawn up between the Plains Indians and the United States Government; and by the time Battiste came to explain what Eagle Woman had told him, almost 30 years later, the Dakotas had lost most of their territory including the Black Hills and Battiste was confined to living on one of the specially designated Indian reservations.

In the year 1856 I, Battiste Good, went to the Black Hills and cried and cried and cried, and suddenly I saw a bird above me which said, 'Stop crying! I am a woman but I will tell you something: My Great Father, Father God who made this place, gave it to me for a home and told me to watch over it. He put a blue sky over my head, and gave me a blue flag to have with his beautiful country.

'Great Father, Father God grew. His flesh was part earth and part stone and part metal and part wood and part water. And he took from them all and placed them here for me and told me to watch over them. I am Eagle Woman who tells you this.

'The whites know that there are four black flags of God; that is to say four divisions of the earth. First he made the earth soft by wetting it, then he cut it into four parts, and one of these parts containing the Black Hills, he gave to the Dakota Indians. And now, because I am a woman, I will not consent to the pouring of blood on this chief house of mine, the Black Hills. The time will come when you will remember my words, for after many years you shall grow up one with the white people.'

Then Eagle Woman circled round and round and gradually passed out of my sight.

155

Then I saw prints of a man's hands on stone, and horse's hoofs and
two thousand years and one hundred million dollars. And I came
away crying as I had gone.
I have told this to many Dakota Indians, and they all agree that it
meant that we were to seek and keep peace with the whites.

Ashnithlai

THE KLIKITAT INDIANS, Washington State, North America

Ashnithlai was a prophet-dreamer of the Washani religion (see page 34).
He lived during the second half of the nineteenth century. All that is
known about him comes from the brief account of his life given by his
niece in 1934.

Until the 1880s Ashnithlai was very much influenced by the white
men's ways and then he had a sudden and devastating visionary experience which completely altered him mentally and physically. From that
time onwards he was recognized as a dreamer.

Like many Indians of the period, Ashnithlai wanted to reassert the
relationship which had once existed between his people and the natural
world. As an old, blind and paralysed man he said, 'Salmon is very good
food. Deer is also good. Camass is good food; also huckleberry and
water. I am showing this that you must be thankful for them.'[3] Within
the simplicity of this statement is contained a declaration of the love that
he felt for the wild and uncultivated earth which had nourished his people
so easily throughout the generations. A famous contemporary of his, a
man called Smohalla who was credited as the leader of the strongly anti-
white Washani movement prevalent after the 1860s, affirmed the same
idea far more forcefully when he said, 'My young men shall never work.
Men who work cannot dream, and wisdom comes to us in dreams. You
ask me to plough the ground. Shall I take out a knife and tear out
my mother's bosom? . . . You ask me to cut grass and make hay and
sell it and be rich like white men. But how dare I cut off my mother's
hair?'[4]

Nothing is known about Ashnithlai's teaching, about what pre-
cipitated his conversion or how much influence he had on his contem-
poraries. But his niece kept a sharp image of the old man she saw one
time in her childhood, and when she told of the things he had prophesied
she began to weep at the memory.

Ashnithlai took over the white man's ways and cultivated the land for
his living. He was not at that time a strong believer in the Washani
religion.
He came home one day with long hip boots. He began to think. At
this time Washani services were being held in the Glenwood district,
and many people were gathered there. At the hour of noon
Ashnithlai said, 'How is this Washani? I am going to sing and dance

as they do, just as a joke.' He began to swing his right arm and dance just as he saw the others do.

Before he knew it he found himself with some unseen strength or power which lifted him off the ground and threw him quite a few feet – just as a child can be tossed.

When he awoke he heard many people singing a Washani song. He heard his own mother and father among those who were singing. Then he began to cry. He was somewhat paralysed and had to crawl on hands and knees.

He cut a pole. He heard a voice speak to him, 'Cut a long pole. You set it up and on this pole we shall descend to you.' He did this. He looked up and saw something coming down the pole. People were landing on the pole without breaking it.

He cried. He tied part of his red blanket to the end of the pole. Then he crawled in the house. He took off his hip boots. His skin came off with the boots. It stuck to the boots and looked as though it had been cooked. The skin peeled off his hands. He had been a mocker of the Washani religion. Now he was singing the song which came to him when he first started to sing and dance. That night he kept on singing his own song.

Some of the neighbours decided they would go and see how he was getting along. That was several nights later. As they drew near they heard 'aaaaaaa-aaaa!' at his dwelling. They thought he was mocking them with his song and his pole and red flag. They laughed.

Ashnithlai knew he had visitors coming, but he was blind and unable to walk. He crawled out to greet his brothers, and when they saw him he was so disfigured that he was no longer the same man.

He said, 'My brothers! I want you to get on your horses and circle my home and this pole seven times. When you enter my house after that also walk around my house seven times.' This they did. Then they shook hands with him. He told his story. 'I am as dead,' he said, 'I must have done a great deal of wrong and an awful sin when I mocked the Washani religion among my people.'

He interpreted what he had seen while he was dead. 'Truly our Indian people are going to be up against something which is very hard. There will be a new law which you will hear like a thunderstorm. A people are coming who will take the strength of thunder. All will be metal and their power taken from the thunder will be metal.'

Tail Feather Woman

THE MENOMINI INDIANS, Wisconsin, North America

In the spring of 1878 considerable excitement was caused in and around Ashland, Wisconsin over a report that Indians were dancing and having powwows further west, and were working their way towards the reservations in this part of the country. I had heard that the party were performing and teaching a new kind of dance, and I resolved to meet them. There were between sixty and seventy in the party which consisted of a young Sioux girl and her interpreter, the balance being made up by Chippewas from the immediate vicinity.[5]

This was Tail Feather Woman. The new religion she taught to the Indians became known as the Dancing Rite, the Drum religion or simply the Powwow. It was adopted by a number of tribes, including the highly conservative Menomini of northern Wisconsin. The Powwow adapted the old dances, beliefs and rituals in such a way that they could survive in a fast-changing world and for several decades it functioned as a vital religious force which enabled the Menomini to maintain their tribal identity and to withstand the influence of the white people. But such resistance did not last indefinitely and when the American anthropologist J S Slotkin came to study the Menomini between 1949 and 1951 he witnessed the fast decay of the Powwow religion. Traditionally the

Menomini were very unwilling to tell or show any of their customs to the whites – they said that they would be killed by the spirits if they did – but they decided independently to ask Slotkin to make a record of their religion in the hope that it would not be forgotten and lost for ever. They said, 'Us Powwow people we ain't got much of us left. All of the old people are all gone now, most of them young people living now. And we are short handed now. We ain't got enough people to fill out the drum organization the way it's supposed to be. The Powwow is going dim all over.'6 And so, Slotkin was able to participate in the rites and question the people on all aspects of their beliefs. Repeatedly he was confronted by apologetic and sad reminiscences about how things should be and once had been. In earlier times there had been much dancing and visionary dreaming, but now it was the beating of the drum, accompanied by songs and a few dances, which was the dominating force at the gatherings.

The person who was most informative was a man called Johnny-The-Thunderer-Comes-With-Noise-Of-Thunder. It is his account of the origin of the Drum which is included here. Tail Feather Woman lay submerged among the reeds for four days. It is an image of the most dreadful isolation, hiding in cold water while every person one knows is killed, and then remaining there, surrounded by the presence of the dead. When the Great Spirit saw the woman he felt pity for her. First he took her to the camp of the white soldiers, and there surrounded but unseen by her persecutors she was given food. Then he gave her the Drum and told her how it was to be used. He told her that the Indians should follow a strict ethical code and attempt to 'do good always'. The Drum and its rituals provided a means of accepting an otherwise unbearable spiritual defeat. The people who followed the religion of Tail Feather Woman were not advocating an attempt to change their situation but rather a means by which they would be able, perhaps, to survive within it – to eat food in the camp of the soldiers without being seen.

I shall narrate a little about how this Dancing Rite Drum came to be. The Great Spirit made everything; it is because of him that there is the Drum.

They who are the white soldiers killed almost all the Sioux in a battle. It was then that the woman, Tail Feather Woman, is said to have hidden among the reeds; in order to breathe there she parted the leaves of the reeds. She probably lay in the water for four days.

When four days had passed it is said that the Spirit then came to her. He probably told her, 'Come, arise'. At that time she thought it was only some person; she did not know that it was the Spirit who was speaking to her. And he told her this.

A little while later she arose from the water. She looked at him; that man standing there above the water. 'It is I. Oh, I pity you!' he told her. 'Arise!' he told her. 'You will go eat; it is I who will take you. Nothing is going to happen to you; it is I who pity you,' that one

probably told her, he who was standing there above the water while she was in the water.

She arose. Then he is said to have taken her to where these white men were eating; he took her there. 'No one will see you. It is I who intend to help you,' he told her. 'Do not be afraid; come with me.' Then she went with that one; he took her there. A big table was there in the white soldiers' camp; one plate was not being used. It is said that he then pointed it out to her, so that she could eat as much as she desired while invisible to the white soldiers. When she was full he took her some place.

She went with him. When she opened her eyes she saw that Drum there. 'Well, then, this is what I give you,' he told her. At that time the Drum probably made a noise, and she saw the drumsticks moving. She heard singing. She listened to them there; at first she heard them singing four songs there.

Well, after this was finished the Spirit spoke to her. He told her everything; he told her how the Indian should perform the Dancing Rite; he gave her to understand how to do everything that is good. He told her the way everyone should act; that they should not be the way they still are – people harming one another, killing one another – no! That was what the Spirit told her.

Now this woman is one to whom the Great Spirit gave it. Therefore is she called 'Tail Feather Woman'; Tail Feather Woman she is named, that woman, the Sioux young woman to whom was given the Drum. She is the one to whom all of it was carefully explained by the Spirit, exactly how the Indian is to live. Everything good was explained to her: that they should pity each other, that they should be good to each other, that they should help each other in everything.

So that Drum was given to that woman. When she took it, she went to her settlement; she went there, taking the Drum there. Then she told those Indians about that Drum. She told them that the Spirit had given it to her. She explained it all to them, and explained the songs to them.

The Great Snake Mumbo

THE LUO AND THE KISII, Kenya, East Africa

The cult of the snake god Mumbo began in 1913 in an area which is now central Nyanza. In spite of the repeated and sometimes drastic steps which were taken to suppress it by the British Administration it was still active in the 1950s. However, apart from this account of the first prophet and leader of the movement, which was written in 1930, very little has been recorded about Mumbo and his followers and any other information has been gleaned from the information in local newspapers.

Certainly the god Mumbo demanded that his followers reject all things European. The cult of Mumbo appealed mostly to the older

people who more readily adapted to the wearing of skins and the renewal of the priests' spiritual authority. There were many variations in the content of Mumbo doctrines, but always it was said that white rule would not last and that a time of plenty would come after its demise.

One evening as Onyango sat in his hut, a gigantic snake appeared, and
swallowed him up. This snake was so big that if it stood upright
with its tail in Lake Victoria, then its head reached into the clouds.
Almost immediately after swallowing him, the snake vomited
Onyango back into his hut. He was frightened but not hurt. The
snake said to him:
'I am the God Mumbo. My two homes are in the Sun and in the Lake.
I have chosen you as the one who must speak for me. Go out and
tell all Africans, especially those who come from Alego, that now I
am their God. Those who I chose personally, and also all those who
acknowledge me will live for ever in plenty. For them the crops will
grow of themselves and there will be no more need to work. I will
cause sheep, cattle and goats to rise up out of the Lake in great
numbers, and they will be given to those who believe in me. All
unbelievers, their families and their cattle, will die.
'I am the God Mumbo and I tell you that the Christian religion is
rotten like a fruit. The practice of making believers wear clothes is
wrong. My followers must let their hair grow long, they must never
cut it. Their clothes shall be the skins of goats and cattle, and they
must never wash. All the white men are your enemies, but the time is

soon coming when they will disappear from our country.

'I must command that daily sacrifices of male cattle, sheep and goats and fowls are made to me. Most of all I prefer black bulls. Have no fear of sacrificing these. I will cause unlimited supplies of black cattle to come to you from the Lango region. My people must now at once kill all their sheep, cattle and goats, and when this is done I will provide them with as many more as they want.'

When he had finished speaking, the Snake disappeared into the Lake. Onyango set about spreading the words of Mumbo to the people, and soon he had many followers. There were those who had been called, and they were mostly the older men, and when they were called they fell into a fit of a trance and spoke strange words, and after that they became the priests of the new religion. These men were reputed to be able to bring the dead back to life and to cure these who were very sick. They would lay the body on the ground, cover it with freshly cut grass, and tie a thick rope around the neck. Then they called upon Mumbo to come and help them in their work.

Those who worshipped Mumbo would stare into the face of the sun at sunrise and sunset, until they were dazzled by it. Then they stretched out their arms towards the sun and prayed. Occasionally they also prayed to the Lake, and sacrificed cattle, throwing the meat into the Lake of the Crocodiles.

The Rastafarians

JAMAICA, West Indies

With the use of the herb you can exist in this dismal state of reality that now exists in Jamaica. You cannot change man, but you can change yourself by the use of the herb.[7]

In 1930 Ras Tafari was crowned as the Negus of Ethopia. He took for himself the name Haile Selassie (Might of the Trinity), and to this the titles King of Kings and Lion of the Tribe of Judah were added. He declared that he was the direct descendant of King Solomon, thus giving himself a genealogical link that stretched back to the first man created by God and placed in Paradise.

In Jamaica this event took on a special significance. People recalled the words of Marcus Garvey, the Jamaican evangelist who was one of the first to assert the heritage and ancestry of all dispossessed blacks whose past had been obliterated by slavery. In 1916, just before his departure for the United States, Garvey had said, 'Look to Africa for the crowning of a Black King; he shall be the Redeemer'.[8] The crowning of Haile Selassie was seen as the fulfilment of this prophecy; it marked the end of an era and it promised the hope of redemption. People turned to the Bible and there they found numerous justifications for the belief that the new king had indeed been sent by God to set them free from their long exile in the white men's world. The Book of Revelation announced the coming of the Lion of the Tribe of Judah, the King of Kings; the prophecies of Daniel described the Ancient of Days as a black man, 'whose garment was white as snow, and the hair of his head like unto pure wool . . . whose feet were like in colour to polished brass'.[9] A new religious mythology evolved around the black king and his legendary African kingdom, a mythology which gave the one-time slaves of Jamaica a past ancestry and a future destiny. They said that Haile Selassie was the living God, the messiah sent to save them. They said that they were the true Israelites of the Bible and that Jamaica was Babylon and hell on earth; and soon the day would come when they would be able to return to their lost homeland. They said that now they knew that the whites were an inferior race; and soon they would lose their power and the blacks would rule the world.

The Rastafarian movement began during the Depression of the 1930s, a time when people felt most severely the pain of their servitude and when they were most in need of some hope of salvation. To escape persecution by the Jamaican Government authorities a group of between 500 and 1,600 Rastafarians went to live in a commune in the hills behind Kingston. It was there during the 1940s and early 1950s that the characteristics of the movement were established. The Rastamen grew their hair long in imitation of the Ethiopian warriors. They cultivated their own crops and lived according to strict codes of diet, cleanliness and dress. It was during this time that marijuana – ganja, the Herb – was cultivated widely and used in all the rituals of meditation.

In 1954 the commune was destroyed by the police and a race of wild-looking, religious ascetics came down into the city slums of Kingston. They established themselves in an area known as Shanty Town and started a new sort of ghetto life, denying any allegiance to the white authorities and living on the edge of utter poverty. They gathered an ever increasing number of converts; and in spite of attempts to suppress it, the movement survived and grew so that when Jamaica gained independence in 1962 Rastafarianism had become the movement of all the urban poor.

Today there are an estimated 100,000 Rastafarians in Jamaica and many from other countries claim to belong to the movement. The true Rastamen still live according to their strict moral codes; and they use the Herb in a similar way to that of the North American Indians with their peyote cactus. Through their smoking the Rastafarians gain access to a spiritual realm where they are no longer oppressed.

'We are in the upper room. That is why Rastaman find such joy.'[10]
In the days of old the prophet, priest, prince, he was always given
  meat, and baskets of bread, and talents of silver for the great works
  done. Now give me love with a parcel of Herbs, and I will do the
  work of works.

Solomon asked for Herbs, for Wisdom, for Knowledge. The Herb is
for the healing of the Nation; the green grass of the field is for the
beast. The Herb was the first wisdom given to Solomon, the first
plant in the garden. The Herb is our only comfort.

Our biggest trouble is to make Herbs free. Herbs have never been
free since I was a slave, and now they step it up. Now we speak the
word – in the Beginning was the Word – and now we wait, we wait.

Herb is our main need, not rum. Herb keeps you vigorous with power
to negotiate and to love. That thing is a loving thing. If all men
smoke it there would be peace; accidents and war are for drunkards.
The Herb is a good thing. It is angel food. The Herb is for peaceful
meditation, not for war.

The Herb is a healer of nations, and needed for meditation. The more
we draw our pipe the more joy comes. When we smoke our Herbs
we are conscious. We are a conscious people. So much so that they
fear us. We do our work. Draw our Herbs. That is all.

Herbs is incense burning in an incensor. The most precious of our
treasures in the earth and under the sun is the Herbs given for healing.

It is so strong in our hearts, its preciousness, that we go to prison and we say, 'It is righteousness and it is mine!' Then they ask me in prison, 'Is it dangerous to use such medicine?' and I say to them, 'Yes, and I do, and I love it'.

What we are dealing with is the right thing. We have decided to bear anything. It is a righteous and religious cause. No other religion knows this yet. The Government knows what we say is true; that's why they persecute us so. We are the true Israelites. When Haile Selassie became Emperor we knew that he was the Messiah. Jesus Christ could not save us; Jesus Christ is a thing of the past. Haile Selassie is the architect and builder of life. He is the King of all Ages. He is the once and future King. In his right hand is lightening and in his left hand is thunder.

> Rasta Fari is man shepherd
> Man shall not want
> For he maketh man
> To lie down in green pastures
> Leave oh leave us not alone
> Thou art man shepherd
> Man shall not want
> Selassie is man rock
> King of Jerusalem
> Who seated up upon the throne of David
> And established out of Zion

We suffer every pangs that a man should not suffer. This land is like a prison to us and when we leave this land it will be like a desolate wilderness. If Rastas did not exist in Jamaica it would sink into the sea and volcanoes and hurricanes would attack it. We want to repatriate to our own land, to Zion. Everything will live in Zion. When we return we will crown him again. Crown him! Crown him! Haile Selassie. King of Kings, Lord of Lords and Conquering Lion. We are the true Israelites. Everything will live in Zion. The man who makes fish will make more fish. Everything there is flourishing, flourishing, flourishing.

The Lord never has the majority on his side, always the minority. The majority has to go the way of destruction. Brimstone and fire for the Western World! Melt the White House Now! Kill Johnson Now! England must burn with fire; it is a wicked place. Britain will become naked and dead, burnt with fire. The rulers of the white world are killing each other. Do not follow the courthouses, the doctors, the teachers, the ministers, the preachers. Curse them! They will fake you to death. Truly. Even if God appear to them they get scared and run. We hate the ways of them that go in the way of wrong. Not their person, but their ways.

Kelevi and the Roses of Life

THE FIJIANS, Big Kandavu Islands, Fiji

> You see Kelevi, sir, but Kelevi is just the container. It is really Jesus Christ who is speaking to you.[11]

Kelevi was the prophet, medicine-man and leader of a small Fijian village. All the people there had given up going to the local Methodist Church which previously had an attendance rate of almost one hundred per cent and instead they went to Kelevi's Houses of Religion. These five native houses were grouped closely together at the foot of a hill. In the centre there was an enclosure built of reeds. On a platform, about a foot below the top, was the chair on which Kelevi sat and from which he directed his religious services. On the rise of the hill a large imposing building had been erected, and here lived Kelevi with his wife and most of the young unmarried girls of the village who were called the Roses of Life.

A service was conducted at six o'clock every morning. Hymns were sung from the Methodist hymn book; prayers were addressed to Jehovah and Christ. Then there was a sermon based on a passage read from the Bible and the people confessed their sins. Then they went out to work.

Kelevi declared that the Methodists were false. He said that they worshipped a great snake who was Satan and who was also the old Fijian god Degei, the one who lived in a cave in the middle of the main island. Kelevi knew these things because he was believed to be the vessel of Jesus Christ and when he spoke, Christ spoke through him.

Kelevi could neither read nor write but he possessed several exercise books which had been written down according to his dictation. These books contained lists of the names of the Roses, the names of the followers and the prayers and laws of the new religion (known as the Good News Written by the Word). They also contained a description of the sins committed by the people and the visions seen by the Roses. The missionary A C Cato, who met Kelevi in 1942 and again in 1947, was given access to these books, and it is from them, and from the conversations that he had with Kelevi and his followers and Roses, that this account is taken.

I am a member of Kelevi's society. I was sick, and Kelevi cured me. When I was cured I desired to be a member of his religion. We who were sick were breathed on. Kelevi breathed on me. The Roses were singing while I was breathed on.

Kelevi says that God speaks to him and he hears him. When all the Roses are present Kelevi stands on the table and chooses the Roses while they are seated. Kelevi wears long trousers and shoes. He spits on the floor and the girls must wipe up his spittle with their hands. If they use paper or a piece of cloth they will not be admitted as true Roses. Kelevi said that the village of the Roses was to be with him. Then the house was built at Utonigau and the Roses lived with Kelevi. One girl became pregnant. Her name was Salote.

One day Kelevi ordered that all the people of the village should gather together in one house. He said that kava should be prepared and the ceremony concerning-useful-work should be performed. This was to help Kelevi appoint an assistant in his work. Strangers were forbidden to enter, and we, the people of the village, were forbidden to speak about it. Kava was brought out to offer at the ceremony before the face of the four winds. Kelevi prayed:

> Source of Life
> Roses of Life
> Kelevi the Speedy
> The End of Time
> The Winged Eagles underneath God

He said, 'Here, sirs, is the kava bowl. I ask that my work be prepared to be set up on Friday week. Be gracious enough to send the works of my request to the Lord of the Source of Life.' Then the people who had gathered, men and women, said, 'e dina, e mana, sa dina'.

One day Kelevi told us to go and wait in the Houses of Religion for three days and three nights, after which the voice of God would be heard. We waited but we did not hear the voice of God. Sometimes Kelevi goes to many places and says that he goes to bring female devils that they might enter the Roses. I saw the devils enter into nine of the girls. Their bodies appeared to shake, their voices became hoarse, and their eyeballs looked strange. When they were like this the Bible was given to them to preach in the Houses of Religion.

Kelevi says, 'I am the greatest Minister of Christ under the sun. I am Christ's greatest Judge under the sun. I am Christ's greatest School-master under the sun. My name is Source of Life. The first man to be Christ's vessel is Kelevi. My work is found in the Book of Revelation – to cause old things to pass away.

'I cannot read. I left Paradise to come here. I conducted the Court of Hell. I judged those who had excuses, from those in the lowest depths of Hell, to those who had just been buried in the world.

'I was in Paradise and I saw the prayers offered in this world were not fulfilled there. In Paradise I saw a Methodist Minister. He was praying. I asked him who sat on the throne in the ocean of glass and why the prayers of the people were rejected. He said, "I pray, I pray, God grant that we may be blessed by the great snake Degei". He was praying to the snake Degei, lying in his cave, he was asking the snake to be the god of the Methodists. This is why prayers offered in this world are not fulfilled. The Minister was praying in order to give life to the great snake and cause the death of the people of Fiji.'

The Road to the Land of the Dead

THE MENOMINI INDIANS, Wisconsin, North America

They say that when a man dies he must make a journey to the west. He follows the Milky Way which is called the road of the dead, and it is a fine road to look at, decorated with brightly coloured flowers. When he arrives at a certain place Little Wolf is waiting for him. Little Wolf has 'prepared a place over there for them Indians. He got some water, whenever Indians get there he wash them, clean them up good; take out everything that's bad. When he's through he let them go. That dead person he's alright, no sickness. Everlasting life is there. Every night they have a dance and have a good time. That Little Wolf he pound the drum all night, make Indians dance every night and have a good time. No more sick, nothing.' [12] A man who has lived badly is sent in another direction, to 'a kind of swamp, water and lots of mud', but not much is said about this place.

This is the traditional belief of the Menomini Indians who today belong to the Powwow religion. They are very strict in their isolationism and it is impossible for a member of the Powwow to have any dealings with the white men or the Catholic religion which the white men brought with them. The story given here is about an Indian who was perhaps a Catholic or at any rate 'joining with them'. It is a simple parable.

A man 'dies' and he expects to travel along the road of the dead which has always been travelled by his people. Instead he finds himself on an unfamiliar road, forced to make impossible decisions and confronted by insurmountable obstacles. It is not only that the landscape is strange to him. Instead of being welcomed by the ruler of the land of the dead, he and the other Catholic Indians who are with him and in the same predicament, are confronted by a white man with a stick who pushes them away. The moral to be drawn from this story is that the Indians must stay with the ways that belong to them – must stay with the Drum religion. The narrator is Johnny-The-Thunderer-Comes-With-Noise-Of-Thunder, the same man who told the Menomini account of Tail Feather Woman and the origin of the Drum religion.

I was dead not long ago; I was dead. I must have been dead all
   night. When I come to all my flesh was just ice cold. Well, I must
   have been dead.
I know I got up, stand. I was standing outside. I knew I was dead
   and I began to look for that trail of the dead they talk about all the
   time. I look but finally I see some kind of a trail, so I follow that for
   a little ways.
And when I come to a place there where those roads fork, I didn't
   know what to do. So I follow one of them trails. And I come to a
   place. Oh I see a lot of Indians. And I look to them Indians;
   they're all Catholics, people I used to know round here in Keshena;

all of them old people and young people, all sitting around there.
And I looked around there and I seen that stairway. That stairway is
all decorated with flowers, and it looks nice and clean; stairway going
towards heaven. But it must be about six foot above the ground,
that's where that stairway was hanging.

And them Indians you know, they want to go to heaven. They
couldn't make it. Some of them they reach the stairway, and they're
trying to start, to go to heaven, you know. I seen somebody
coming down the steps there; he had that long stick; he pushes them
Indians off. He says, 'You don't belong here; you ain't supposed to
come here. You Indian why don't you follow that other trail?
That's where you belong.' That looks like a white man taking
charge of that stairway.

I seen quite a few Indian people there, trying to go up towards that
stairway. But that white man, you know, he push them off. He tell
them, 'You can't go over there. You got a place to go. You don't
belong here. That's what that Great Spirit boss of yours told me to
tell you.'

And this fellow called me up and I got on that stairway and visited him. He asked me where I belonged. He said, 'See that Medicine Lodge Hall that's where you belong, not here. Only white people get through here. You Indians, you are supposed to take the other trail. And you got that religion there, the Medicine Dance, and the Drum. That's where you belong. That's where you're supposed to go. Not here.'

The Yakan Water Cult

THE LUGBARA, Uganda, East Africa

The Lugbara drank the Yakan water to protect themselves from danger. They used it first in warfare and then against sickness. When the Yakan water cult was at its height at the beginning of this century, they believed not only that the water would protect them from bullets but that it would also enable the world to be transformed into a perfect place where there was no more death. Today the magical water is still used as a means of curing people suffering from certain diseases.

The Yakan water came from a pool in Ajebi in Kakwa country which borders on Lugbaraland. No matter how much the Yakan water was diluted its sacred qualities did not diminish. It was distributed and sold by the priests of the cult; and it was said that they mixed it with some of the juice of a plant called 'the lion bulb' which, if used in large quantities, could induce a state of frenzy.

Many warlike tribal peoples adopted protective magic to help fight the sudden invasion of the white men with their diseases and weapons. But the Yakan water cult was distinguished by the fact that under the leadership of the Kakwa prophet Rembe it became institutionalized as a political and religious force. A new hierarchy of priests was established and a people who previously had been antagonistic to each other were united by their shared beliefs and aspirations. In this way they were able to leave the rigid social structures of their past and adapt themselves more to their present.

The Lugbara had maintained an isolated existence until the end of the nineteenth century when they were suddenly confronted by the encroaching forces of a changing outside world. There came wave upon wave of deadly epidemics which killed the people and their cattle, and around 1900 Europeans and Arab slave traders arrived in their territory. The Lugbara believed that any change imposed on their society was due to the remote creative force known as Spirit; and he upset the basic stability of their existence only when he was dissatisfied with them in some way. So, the diseases, the invasions, the famines and the changes in the ecological system were all evidence of Spirit's anger. And the white men with their guns and their strength were seen as direct emissaries sent by Spirit. The people needed help from equally powerful but benevolent supernatural forces; and this help was offered to them by the prophet

Rembe, a diviner, a healer of sicknesses who was sent by Spirit.

Rembe's first exchange with the Lugbara was in 1890 when he had
'bought' some magical water from another Sudanese tribe and sold it to
the eastern Lugbara who were then fighting against the troops of
Emin Pasha. He said that by drinking the water they would be victorious
in battle. When this prediction proved correct his reputation was won.
The Lugbara sent messengers to see Rembe at Ajebi to learn his teachings, to consult his oracle and to bring back the precious water from the
pool. In 1914 they invited him to come and visit them. He spent several
months travelling through the region, dispensing water, setting up
sacred meeting places and instructing the new chiefs of his cult. His
main concern was to bring an end to fighting among the Lugbara themselves and to cure sickness. The priests of the cult gained added status
because they alone were felt to be strong enough to deal with the white
men; and it was they, and not the traditional rainmakers, who presented
themselves to the British Administration to act as intermediaries.

However, by 1916 when diseases and political upheavals were
becoming more and more disruptive, the medical and essentially pacifist
aspect of the cult was superceded by more revolutionary aims and the
anti-white feeling became predominant. It was at this stage that the cult
members began their military marches and their frenzied imitations of
colonial behaviour. In 1919 the British Authorities decided to put a stop
to the movement with its frequent large gatherings and its underlying
mood of angry hysteria. Many leaders of the cult including Rembe
were arrested and executed, and from that time onwards its political
energy was broken. Today Rembe is still remembered as a mythological
hero and saviour of the people and the power of Yakan water is still
used to cure certain sicknesses which possess a man with fits of trembling.

Rembe was a little man, but he was like a king. When he sat here
everyone would gather to hear his words. His words were great and
many. He called men and all came to him.
Is Rembe dead? Where is his grave. We have never heard how he
escaped or where he died. Perhaps he is still alive. If he were
locked up he would always escape. He had an iron anklet on his right
leg, and they tied him to a wall by this, but he escaped. He was our
Agent. He had soldiers and parades and a tall pole called the *a'bi*, on
top of which sat a man. We still look for him. Where did he go?
Rembe said, 'I placed here my a'bi tree, the tree planted on a grave.
Let people come here with food and beer and let them dance their
death dance here. This tree is now your tree.'
He gave us the a'bi tree so we did not refuse it. It helped us. My
father became like a Sultan of Yakan and he distributed the water of
Yakan given to him by Rembe. Rembe walked through Lugbaraland
and put those trees everywhere, in Maraca, in Terego, in Kijomoru,
everywhere. Then people came to the tree, and gave food and wealth

to the 'chief' there. They came from all Maraca, and also other men. In the evening they danced. The dance was called 'to dance *yakan* at the foot of the a'bi tree'.

The water came from the pool at Ajebi. In the pool lived a snake called Dede, the grandmother-who-protects-us-from-evil. This snake was like a python but with many colours. Some say it was half man and half water snake. Perhaps it was a great monitor lizard. The snake knew the words of the Yakan cult, and it told us that we should drink Yakan water so as not to be sick. All the words of Yakan came from that snake Dede.

The people who drank the water believed that it would preserve them from death. They said that now their ancestors would come to life; that they could defy government orders and need not pay tax. They said that now they could not be hurt by the rifles of the white man because now those rifles would only shoot water. They themselves would be provided with rifles so that they could drive the white men out of their country. Those rifles would perhaps be brought up river by a spirit called Jeremani the German. Any man who refused to drink the water became a termite when he died, or he was carried away by a strong wind.

People went slowly to Kakwa, to Kuku country, to Yudu the clan of Rembe. He gave them a little pot of water. Then they returned with it. They brought it to Udupi, others to Oluvu, Maraca, every man bought his own. Then they called together many people, men, girls and children, all drank the water. They wanted to refuse the words of the white men. They thought, and every man came with arrows, and bracelets and even rupees with which to buy this water. And girls, if big, they lay down at the drinking place with the soldiers who collected the money and those things to pay for the Yakan water. Every morning they made a parade, like the police do at Arua. Then people brought food and chickens and beans and groundnuts, and simsim and millet and sorghum; every person took those things when buying the water.

Rembe brought water to say, 'Stay quiet and do not fight your friends'. The people refused because of the Europeans and said, 'The white men came to destroy our land'. Rembe said, 'Let us stay here in peace, without fighting, and let the white men go back to their own country'. Rembe said, 'The water I have given to you and which you have drunk, will give you one heart. Now you are all of one heart. I do not want fighting again. I want you all to be with cooled hearts.' Those were the words of Rembe.

We did not know the white men and we feared them. Rembe came to show us that they were people. He showed us how to fight against them and not to fear them and their strength. When the white men heard of these matters they arrested the sellers of water and sent them to prison, and some of them died there.

fili

kalsi

yizu

kedilka

Abel and Hallelujah

THE AKAWAIO, Guyana, South America

Bichiwung went to England (see page 70), and, as a result of his meeting with God and his revelation about the true Indian religion he became the prophet leader of Hallelujah among the Makusi. Many neighbouring peoples came to learn his songs and the doctrines of his new religion; and Hallelujah was practised by a number of tribes living where the frontiers of Venezuela, Brazil and Guyana meet. However, when the missionaries became more influential in their teaching, the religion was usually overrun and it is only among the Akawaio that it has survived until the present day as an influential and flourishing religion. The man who brought Hallelujah to the Akawaio was a shaman called Abel.

Like Bichiwung, Abel was determined to see God for himself. He tried to do so during his magical spirit flights and he tried to find him when he walked alone in the mountains. When these traditional methods failed him, he tried praying. It was through the dream visions arising out of his prayers that he was taken up to heaven where he was able to meet God and to speak with him in order to learn more about Hallelujah.

The natural ambivalence which the Indians felt towards the white men was resolved within the framework of Hallelujah with its fusion of the old Indian beliefs and certain aspects of Christian teaching. Abel meets not only Noah and God in Heaven, but also jaguar, wild animals, nature spirits, angels and archangels who pray and play on their mouth organs. This complex host of characters are all united as they dance the Hallelujah dances.

Abel died some time around the first decade of this century. His youngest daughter was still alive when this account of his vision of heaven was collected in 1957.

Abel got Hallelujah from Bichiwung. He didn't get it directly from him, but he used to dream and his spirit went up to heaven; then he used to wake up and tell the people they must believe because it was good, so he used to get Hallelujah directly.

Abel slept six days, then he got Hallelujah from God. He slept for almost a week and his wife and children were crying. They blocked up the path to heaven which is like a big sea, so that he couldn't get past it.

He said to them on waking up that they mustn't cry when someone died, otherwise the dead can't get to heaven. The mourner must just pray. After the body is put in the grave the people can cry, but not before.

Abel tried to get to God. He prayed and thought and sought for God, but could not find Him. Three times he went in spirit to heaven, but he met only Indians. Eventually he got to the gates of heaven but the door was closed. He knocked but could not get in. Then the door opened a little and God said, 'What do you want?'

Abel said to God, 'I want you'.

God said, 'No, you come as Indian, you have to wait until you have died; you have sinned'.

Abel wanted to find out where Hallelujah came from. He kept dreaming in order to find it. He wanted to look for it in heaven but couldn't pass because of the great wind. When he was dreaming he saw animals, howler monkey, jaguar and others in the path. When he was dreaming a second time he found a big sea. He passed that and he found spirits with good musical instruments. These spirits had their own Hallelujah but he didn't bother about that.

Then Abel dreamt again and he saw a river, somewhere in England perhaps, but he didn't know where. Then he saw a big village. Then he found Noah. Noah had a big boat and Abel saw many animals in this boat.

Abel dreamt again and then his spirit walked on the trail. He saw one trail which went to the east and one which went to the west. He followed the eastern trail. He climbed a hill and found many people dancing Hallelujah there and he joined them. While they were dancing he saw a big gourd come on its own, without being carried. Everyone drank from it. Before he got some of the gourd which came in front of him it went away.

Abel dreamt again that he saw a door open in front of him. He tried to go in but the door closed leaving a small hole. He prayed – while he was still sleeping all this time – and he got his head through only. He saw all sorts of things. He didn't want to return to earth after seeing all the nice things there.

He had another dream. His spirit was told that if the Indians followed Hallelujah always they would have white people as their servants. If they did not they would become the servants of the white people. He told the people this and also said that the priests would come, and they must not believe what the priests said, but must keep to Hallelujah.

The God Peyote

THE DELAWARE INDIANS, Oklahoma, North America

They say, 'Knowledge of Peyote can be had only by eating Peyote'. They say that this small cactus plant, the 'diabolic root' which grows in northern Mexico and southern Texas, is a god who reveals himself and his doctrines and bestows his healing powers on those who participate in his ceremonies.

Until the middle of the nineteenth century peyote was known only among certain Mexican Indian tribes who used it as part of their magical cult ceremonies. Then it was adopted, first by the Kiowa in the 1870s, and later by the Comanches, the Delawares and other tribes of the Plains. Peyotism was quickly established as an important new religion which provided cultural unity and dignity to peoples who were in danger of total spiritual annihilation. The visions induced by peyote enabled people to rediscover their contact with the spirit forces without recourse to the complex ceremonies and priesthood which were no longer possible within the restrictions of reservation life.

Peyotism is a religion of acceptance and resignation. Its worshippers, unlike the participants in the Ghost Dance, do not strive to achieve visions of the return of a better and happier world, nor do they wait with urgent anticipation for the time when the white man will be removed from their land. Instead each individual attempts to achieve a spiritual state of transcendence and quiet which cannot be reached or destroyed by any interference from the outside world.

The Delawares were one of the few tribes able to maintain a distinct cultural unity by the use of peyote in what was known as the Big House ceremony. However, even when this study of them was made in 1929–30, it was feared that the younger generation would have no more use for the wisdom given by the god Peyote.

The Big House ceremony was performed in the second tepee. The worshippers would sit in a circle around the central, half-moon-shaped altar, and for 12 to 18 hours they would eat the peyote buttons to the accompaniment of singing, drum beats and the sound of rattles shaking. Within the strong religious framework of the meeting all the visions and trances induced by the drug were related to the spirit forces of earth, air, water and to the presence of the Great Spirit – Earthmaker, the god of all things.

There are many legends which tell how the plant and its uses were first discovered. Always there is the central theme of one person, lost, helpless and cut off from all human contact to whom the god Peyote comes to bring comfort and relief. The old Comanche woman is the 'lost one' in this account given by the Delawares in 1930; but others tell of a warrior or a young boy who found themselves similarly stranded and without hope. In descriptions of the individual visions experienced by the users of peyote there is always this effort to reach such a state of oneness with god and man that all the fears and uncertainties of the world are lifted: 'I prayed to Earthmaker. I bowed my head and closed my eyes and began to speak. As I prayed I was aware of something above me, and there he was: Earthmaker, to whom I was praying, he it was. Now this is what I felt and saw. All of us sitting there, we had altogether one spirit or soul, at least that is what I learnt. Whatever I thought of I immediately knew. If I thought of a certain place, far away, immediately I was there. I was my thought.'[13]

About seventy-five years ago the Comanche Indians were at war with some Mexican Indian tribes. Once after having successfully raided their enemies they were pursued so closely that they were forced to leave behind one of their women who had been sick for a long time,

178

and had become so exhausted that she asked to be left behind.
They provided this woman with shelter, food and medicine and left
with her a little boy to take care of her needs, and then they
continued their flight westwards. It was their intention to return for
her as soon as they could evade their pursuers. They knew that the
other Indians, their enemies, would not harm the old woman and
the little boy, for it is the custom of the Indians not to kill any
woman or child left behind under such conditions. However, the
little boy was anxious to follow his people, and when darkness fell
he ran away from the sick woman, and following the tracks of the
horses he tried to catch up with the band. The boy followed the
trail until he was too tired to go any farther, and then he fell asleep
under the trees somewhere.

As soon as the woman missed him she became troubled, fearing that
he might lose his way or fall by the wayside before he reached his
people. She became so worried that sick as she was she managed to
rise, and she followed him. Weak from sickness and old age, she

hunted for him, praying and pleading with the Great Spirit to spare
him. She told the Great Spirit that she herself would be willing to
die if the child was spared. But after going for a short distance, her
strength left her and she fell unconscious to the ground.

While she was in this state an unknown being came to her. He
appeared to be an Indian, dressed in the manner of the great chiefs
of her own people. Speaking in her own language he said:

'You are sick, old woman, and yet you are more worried about the
child than you are about yourself. Do not worry about him. He is
safe.'

Pointing to the west he said, 'Tomorrow when the sun is high the
boy will reach the camp of his people safely; but unless you have
help and do as I tell you, you will not live long.

'When I have gone, you will find a herb where I am standing. If you
eat this herb you will discover the greatest medicine in this world for
the Indians. After you have eaten it the Great Spirit will teach you
the songs, the rules and regulations of a new Indian religion. I
repeat, when I am gone pull up the plant which will appear where I
now stand, and eat as much as you can.'

While the old woman was looking and listening to this being who
stood before her, the man began to vanish, lowering himself gently
into the ground. She saw in the spot where he had been a number of
strange plants. Around them there was light. She knew from what
she had been told that these were the plants that she must eat in
order to regain her health. She ate as many as she could and
immediately felt her strength returning to her.

After a while the plant itself took the form of a chief and medicine-
man and began to talk. The plant was peyote, and the chief was also
Peyote himself.

Peyote showed the woman the plan of the tepee which all
worshippers were to have when they ate the plant, and he said, 'I
want you to look within this place of worship. You will find a half
moon moulded out of the earth. This represents the altar. Behind it,
as near as possible to the centre, there will be a fireplace. To build
the fire, use the very best wood, selected and specially prepared for
this purpose.'

Then Peyote taught her the four original songs which have to be sung
in the meeting: the opening song of the meeting, the midnight
water-call song, the morning water-call song, and the closing song.
He also instructed her in all the other rules of the meeting.

This is the way Peyote was revealed to the Indians.

We Are All Strangers Here

THE GUNWINGGU ABORIGINES, Arnhem Land, Australia

The following excerpt is from a long monologue by a Gunwinggu-speaking woman living at Oenpelli, in western Arnhem Land, Australia. Gunwinggu speakers moved into this area when the original inhabitants were almost gone as a result of sickness or direct killings, or being drawn towards centres of European settlement as it expanded eastwards.

The narrative refers first to two persons (anthropologists) and what they were doing in the area. The 'First People' are the mythical beings who were responsible for shaping the land and putting within it the ancestors of present-day Aborigines.

To explain why the Gunwinggu-speaking people at Oenpelli had left their lands and seemed to be forgetting them, the narrator tells how at first they were frightened of the white men, and how their children were taken to live in mission dormitories and got used to European food. She is, in fact, saying that this was one of the main reasons why so many Aborigines lived on settlements or in towns and did not return to their own country, and had become dependent on introduced foods and often on alcohol.

The speaker was talking in Gunwinggu to Catherine H Berndt early in 1950. Several years later, the region became the centre of a still-unresolved controversy over uranium-mining projects, something nobody had foreseen. One consequence has been the Aborigines' renewed interest in their own local territories and a desire to return to their homeland.

Those two didn't come here for nothing. They came to learn our
language and our thoughts, and about what happens in the sacred
rituals. They went here and there and saw many different places,
and the people belonging to those places taught them their
languages. Then they came here for us; wanted to see our country,
and what we were doing. They want to learn everything they can
here, all about out language and about the dreaming beings who put
themselves in our country. But we don't go to look after our
country, to see that it is all right – our very own country, where we
were born. We just came here to stay, where today the place belongs
to the white man, but before was the Aborigines'. Now the white
man has it: but we still stay here.
So those two came to let us know about this, to remind us how,
before, we were born in our country: those First People made it
all for us, and made us too, so that we became human, able to speak
and to walk. That is why these two came: for it was only recently
that we came here, where white people had made a camp, and we
tasted that food and tobacco when they introduced it to us. Now
we all want to stay here, we don't go back to live in our own places
where we were born. We just forget that country. We just stay here
so that we can get white man's food. We don't live in our country.

We are all strangers here, except for only a few. We all just came as strangers and saw this place, and saw for the first time the house the 'white' man made – for we, ourselves, make our houses of paperbark and stringybark. Today, we make our houses out of iron, and we go inside any time when it rains. It is only recently that we saw those white people. Before, we didn't know them and we were afraid. We feared them, just as those original people living here did when

BELOW AND RIGHT
Two snapshots from an anonymous photo album which probably dates from the late 1930s, show Australian Aborigines near a central railway station. It is not known where the photograph was taken, nor to what group these people belonged.

they first saw white men making camp here, and going up to the camps to look for children. They ran away in fear, and stayed in the grass. They went in fear into the grass, being frightened when they saw that 'white' body; and they were afraid of guns, too, and the sound of shooting. They didn't stay in the camp. They went about frightened in the middle of the night, when the white man slept after putting out his light. The Aborigines watched that light, looking out for it. And they said, 'Well, he's asleep, that white man, so now we can come out!' They were afraid of that gun; nobody before had made such a noise! They went and lived in the rocks and caves and stayed there. Then, those who had become used to the strangers told the others who were still frightened: 'You don't want to run away in fear! He won't kill you, or shoot you with that gun! He shoots only animals, he eats only their flesh, so don't run away! This man who came, he is the same as us, but these people just became 'white'.'

Time went on; and at last they found children and put them in the dormitory. The original people here got used to staying among white people. And then the new people came: that's when they saw that a white man's body was really 'white'.

Time passed, and our people lost their fear. Some of our people went into the dormitories and slept among the white people, but some of the children ran away. They kept thinking of their fathers and mothers, and they were still afraid of the white man. They said in their minds, 'Perhaps, when we sleep, he will shoot us in the night!' So they ran away. Every morning, that white man went to look for them, and caught them. He kept on doing that. Some he couldn't find, of those young boys and girls; but some, he took their arms. Then they were frightened; they cried loudly when he touched their skin, those children. That child had no sense, because they hadn't explained to him properly. He tried to cry, and urinated in fear when the white man touched his skin. He tried to run away, but those Aborigines standing nearby took hold of him. He tried to bite them; but at last they got a lot of those children and brought them to the dormitory. And they told them not to bite the white man's hand. They said to them, 'You stay quiet with that white man, or he might shoot you with his gun!' Then they slept in the white man's place. He gave them food and said to them: 'Eat it, for the very first time!' He gave them goat's milk too. But they threw away all that milk, and a dog came and ate it all up.

For a long time they were afraid. Then their mothers and fathers brought them fish and wild honey. Time went on, and at last they lost their fear. They tasted the white man's food and meat, and goat's milk; and after a while they all got used to staying here. They didn't go up to the camps to see their mothers and fathers, but just played in that place where they camped with the white man.

TRIBAL LOCATIONS IN AFRICA

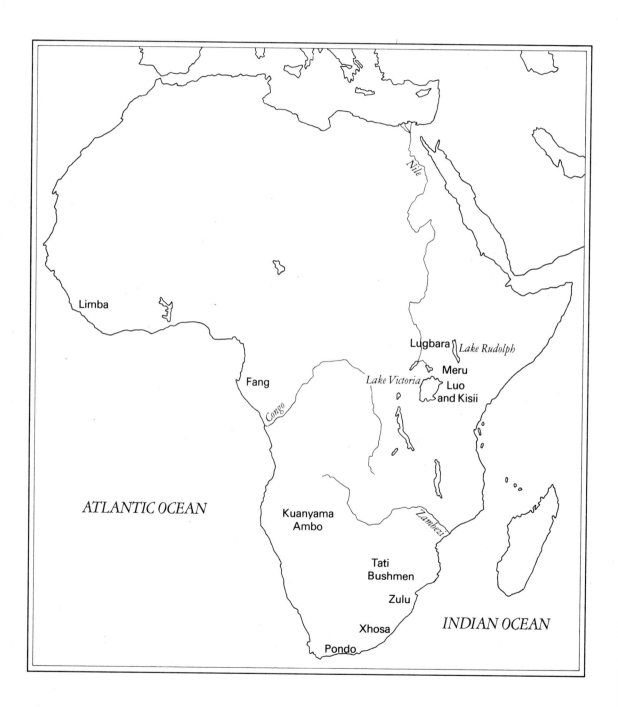

TRIBAL LOCATIONS IN AUSTRALASIA

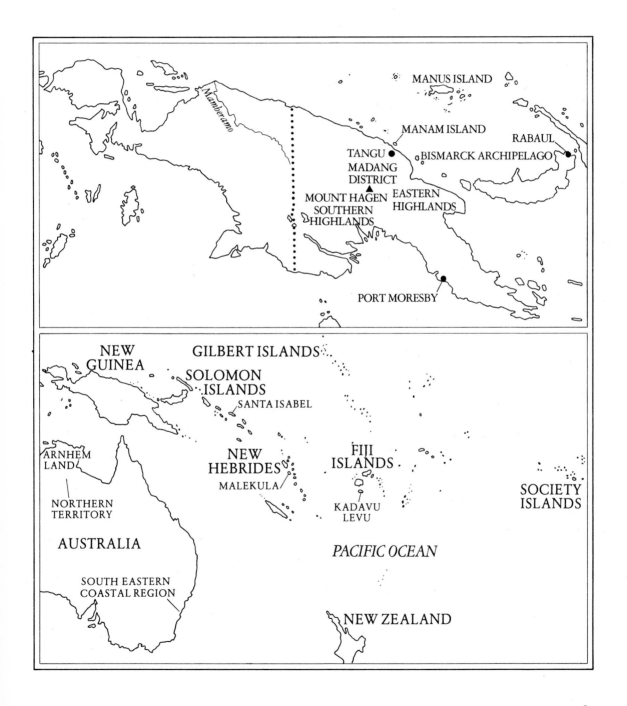

TRIBAL LOCATIONS IN NORTH AMERICA

NOTES

Foreword 1. Herodotus, Fourth Book, chap. 45
2. Levi-Strauss, Claude 'The Scope of Anthropology', *Current Anthropology*, vol. 7, no. 2, April 1966, p. 121
3. Frobenius, L. *The Childhood of Man* 1909, p. 35
4. Rasmussen, Knud Reports of the Fifth Thule Expedition 1921–4, vol. 8, Copenhagen
Introduction 1. Finnegan, Ruth *Oral Literature in Africa*, Clarendon Press, Oxford 1970, p. 311
2. Butt, Audrey 'The Birth of a Religion', *Journal of the Royal Anthropological Institute*, no. 90, part I 1960, p. 72
3. Berndt, R. M. *Surviving Influence of Mission Contact on the Daly River, Northern Territory of Australia*, Neue Zeitschrift für Missionswissenschaft 1952, vol. 8, p. 11
4. *Ibid* p. 13
5. The Book of Revelations, chap. 21, v. 1
6. The Book of Isaiah, chap. 13, v. 10
7. Mooney, James 'The Ghost Dance Religion and the Sioux Outbreak of 1890', Fourteenth Annual Report of the Bureau of Ethnology to the Secretary of the Smithsonian Institute 1892–3, Washington 1896, p. 789
8. Winks, Robin 'The Doctrine of Hau-hauism', *The Journal of the Polynesian Society*, no. 3, 1953, p. 202
9. Berndt, C. H. and R. M. 'An Oenpelli Dialogue: Culture Contact', *Oceania* 1951, vol. 22, no. 1, pp. 28–9
The Arrival 1. Mooney, *op. cit.* p. 961
2. Raven – a supernatural animal who plays an important role in Tlingit mythology.
3. Spier, Leslie 'The Prophet Dance of the North West and its Derivatives', *General Series in Anthropology* 1, 1935, p. 7
4. Du Bois, Cora 'The Feather Cult of Middle Columbia', *General Series in Anthropology* 7, 1938, p. 8
5. Loeb, E. M. 'Ambo Folklore', *Anthropological Records* 1949–52, p. 315
The Secret 1. Callaway, H. *The Religious System of the Amazulu*, Natal 1870
2. Cargo – pidgin word that has come to denote all varieties of goods brought by the white men.
3. Head-he-go-round – pidgin term for the Vailala Madness, a New Guinea cargo movement.
4. Schwarz, Theodore 'The Paliau Movement in the Admiralty Islands, 1946–54' Anthropological Papers of the American Museum of Natural History (New York) 49, Part 2, 1962, p. 249
5. Butt *op. cit.* p. 73
6. *Ibid* p. 72
7. Burridge, K. O. L. *Mambu: a Melanesian Millenium*, Harper reprint 1960, p. 165
Races of Man 1. Mooney *op. cit.* p. 721
2. Wallis, Wilson D. and Ruth Sawtel *The Micmac Indians of Eastern Canada*, University of Minnesota Press, 1955, p. 331
3. Hunter, Monica 'Reaction to Conquest', International African Institute 1936, p. 352, Reprinted 1961
4. *Ibid* p. 232
5. Deacon, A. Bernard *Malekula: a Vanishing People in the New

Hebrides, George Routledge, London 1934, p. xxxii
7. Callaway, *op. cit.* p. 138
8. *Ibid* p. 139
9. *Ibid* p. 139
The Land of the Dead 1. Trilles, P. H. *Les Pygmées de la Fôret Equatoriale*, Anthropes Paris 1931, trans. by Elias Canetti in *Crowds and Power*, Victor Gollancz Ltd, London 1962, p. 42
2. The Book of Revelations, chap. 21, v. 4
3. Du Bois, Cora 'The 1870 Ghost Dance' *Anthropological Records 3*, University of California Press, Berkeley 1939, p. 10
4. Belshaw, Cyril S. 'Recent History of Mekeo Society' *Oceania* 22, 1951, p. 4
5. Du Bois *op. cit.* p. 34
6. Mooney *op. cit.* p. 764
7. *Ibid* pp. 772–3
8. McLuhan, T. C. ed. *Touch the Earth*, New York Pocket Books 1972, p. 77
9. Mooney *op. cit.* p. 1073
10. *Ibid* p. 1072
11. Kafirs – from the Arabic word for infidel, once used to describe African or Bantu people.
12. Assegais – slender spears of hard wood tipped with iron.
13. Greenwood, William 'The Upraised Hand: the Spiritual Significance of the Rise of the Ringatu Faith', *The Journal of the Polynesian Society* 51, 1, 1942, p. 4
14. Lantenari, Vittorio *The Religions of the Oppressed: a Study of Modern Messianic Cults*, trans. Lisa Sergio, Alfred Knopf New York; Macgibbon and Kee London 1963, p. 357
15. Oosterwal, Gottfried 'A Cargo Cult in the Mamberamo Area', *Ethnology* II, 1, 1963, pp. 8 and 11
16. *Ibid* p. 3
17. *Ibid* p. 7
Aftermath 1. Slotkin, J. S. 'Menomini Peyotism: A Study of Individual Variation on a Primary Group with a Homogeneous Culture', Transactions of the American Philosophical Society, N.S. 42, part 4, 1952, p. 580
2. Neihardt, John G. (Ed.) *Black Elk Speaks*, William Morrow New York 1932, p. 77
3. Du Bois, Cora, *General Series in Anthropology* 7, 1938, p. 18
4. Mooney *op. cit.* p. 716
5. Slotkin, J. S. *Menomini Powwow*, Milwaukee Public Museum Publications in Anthropology 4, 1957, Appendix I, p. 155
6. *Ibid* p. 16
7. Wescott, Joan from her field notes made in Jamaica in 1966
8. Barrett, Leonard E. *The Rastafarians*, Heinemann for Sangster's Bookstores Ltd, Kingston 1977, p. 81
9. The Book of Daniel, chap. 7, v. 9
10. Wescott *op. cit.*
11. Cato, A. C. 'A New Religious Cult in Fiji', *Oceania* 18, 1947, p. 147
12. Slotkin *op. cit.* p. 49
13. Petrullo, Vincenzo *The Diabolical Root* University of Pennsylvania Press 1934, pp. 12–13

ACKNOWLEDGMENTS

The Big Bird Comes: arranged by Ronald M. Berndt from his article 'A Cargo Movement in the Eastern Highlands of New Guinea' (*Oceania*, 1952–3, vol. 23, nos 1–3, pp. 50–2, 202–3)

The Wagons that Died: 'The Tati Bushmen and their Language' by S. S. Dornan (Journal of the Royal Anthropological Institute 1917, no. 47, p. 84) Reprinted by courtesy of the Royal Anthropological Institute of Great Britain and Ireland

La Pérouse at Lituya Bay: slightly abridged from 'Under Mount Saint Elias: The History and Culture of the Yakutat Tlingit Indians' by F. de Laguna (*Smithsonian Contributions to Anthropology* vol. 7, Part 1, 1972, pp. 258–9) Reprinted by permission of the Smithsonian Institute Press, Washington D.C.

The Big-house-Ship: slightly adapted from *The Booandik Tribe of South Australia* by Mrs James Smith (published by the South Australian Government, 1880, p. 7)

The Washani Religion: 'The Feather Cult of Middle Columbia' by Cora du Bois (*General Series in Anthropology* 1938, vol. 7, p. 8)

Something Strange is Creeping across the Waters: 'Ambo Folklore' by E. M. Loeb (*Anthropological Records*, University of California Press vol. 13, no. 4, pp. 317–19)

The Man who Saw them First and *How Snakes Crawl inside the Women:* arranged by Ronald M. Berndt from his article 'A Cargo Movement in the Eastern Highlands of New Guinea' (Oceania, 1952–3, vol. 23, nos 1–3, pp. 50–2, 203–5)

The Coming of the Wasichu: slightly adapted from *Black Elk Speaks* edited by John G. Neihardt (Simon & Schuster Pocket Books Edition, © John G. Neihardt 1932, 1959, 1961)

The Landing of Mendana: slightly adapted from 'Santa Isabel, Solomon Islands', by G. Bogesi (*Oceania*, 1947–48, vol. 24, pp. 354–5)

Ongka's Narrative: Ongka by Andrew Strathern (Duckworth, London and New York 1978, chap. 1, pp. 11–12)

Mambu Goes to Australia: slightly adapted from 'Cargo Cult Activity in Tangu' by K. O. L. Burridge (*Oceania*, 1953–4, vol. 24, no. 4, pp. 245–6) Reprinted by permission of the author and *Oceania*

The Day of the Crocodiles: translated and abridged by Julia Blackburn from 'Proverbes, Légendes et Contes Fang' by P. H. Trilles (*Bulletin de la Société Neuchateloise de Géographie* 1902–3, tome 14, pp. 141–53)

Paliau and Jesus: slightly adapted from 'The Paliau Movement in the Admiralty Islands' by Theodore Schwartz (*Anthropological Papers of the American Museum of Natural History* 1962, vol. 49, part 2, pp. 256–8) By permission of the author and the American Museum of Natural History

The Red Man: slightly abridged from 'The Coming of the Red Foreigners into the Wiru Area' by Robert M. Paia (*Oral History* 1977, vol. 5, no. 4, pp. 51–3) Reprinted by courtesy of the Institute of Papua New Guinea Studies

A New Dreaming for the Aborigines: arranged by Ronald M. Berndt from his article 'Surviving Influence of Mission Contact on the Daly River' (Neue Zeitschrift für Missionswissenschaft 1952, vol. 8, parts 2–3, pp. 1–15, 16–20) Reprinted by permission of the publisher

Bichiwung Goes to Engiland: selected and slightly adapted from 'The Birth of a Religion' by Audrey Butt (*Journal of the Royal Anthropological Institute* 1960, no. 90, part 1, pp. 69–71, 74–7) Reprinted by courtesy of the Royal Anthropological Institute of Great Britain and Ireland and the author

Berebi and the Shivering Poison: arranged by Ronald M. Berndt from his article 'Reaction to Contact in the Eastern Highlands of New Guinea' (*Oceania* 1954, vol. 24, nos 3 and 4, pp. 190–228, 255–74)

Houses Bulging with Cargo: slightly abridged from 'Cargo and Inflation in Mount Hagen' by Andrew Strathern (*Oceania* 1970–1, vol. 41, no. 4, pp. 258–260)

Tuman and Ambwerk: slightly abridged from *Mambu* by K. O. L. Burridge (Methuen, London 1960; Harper & Row, New York 1960, pp. 155–160) Reprinted by permission of A. D. Peters & Company Limited

Gluscap (the Man made First) and Hadam: slightly abridged from 'Micmac Folklore' by Elsie Crews Parsons (*Journal of American Folklore* 1925, vol. 28, pp. 88–90) Reprinted by permission of the American Folklore Society

Macassar White Man and Dog: slightly adapted from *A Black Civilization* by W. Lloyd Warner (Harper & Row, New York 1937 & 1965) Reprinted by permission of Harper & Row, Publishers Inc

Uthixo and Adam and Eve: Reaction to Conquest in a South African Tribe by Monica Hunter (International African Institute London 1936, pp. 351–2) Reprinted by permission of the International African Institute and the author

Why Men Became Black: slightly adapted from *Malekula: A Vanishing People in the New Hebrides* by Bernard Deacon

(Routledge, London 1934, pp. 723–5) Reprinted by permission of Routledge & Kegan Paul Limited

The Shawnee Indians and the Master of Life: The Life of Tecumseh by Benjamin Drake (E. Morgan, Cincinnati 1841, pp. 21–2)

The Woman who Mated with a Dog: 'The Intellectual Culture of the Iglulik Eskimos' by Knud Rasmussen (Reports of the Fifth Thule Expedition, Copenhagen vol. 8, p. 227)

The Indian who Danced: slightly abridged from 'Pueblo Indian Folk Tales' by A. M. Espinosa (*Journal of American Folklore* 1936, vol. 49, pp. 118–19) Reprinted by permission of the American Folklore Society

We Thought We Possessed All Things: slighly abridged from *The Religious System of the Amazulus* by Rev. H. Callaway (Natal 1870, pp. 137–9)

Kanu and the Book: Limba Stories and Storytelling by Ruth Finnegan (Oxford University Press 1967, pp. 261–3) Reprinted by permission of Oxford University Press

All People Come from the Same Place: from *The Mugwe: A Failing Prophet* by B. Bernardi (Oxford University Press 1959, pp. 193–4) Reprinted by permission of the author

Adam and Riva in Devil-Devil Country: arranged by Ronald M. Berndt from 'Surviving Influence of Mission Contact on the Daly River' (Neue Zeitschrift für Missionswissenschaft 1952, vol. 8, parts 2–3, pp. 16–20)

The Noise: from *New Lives for Old* by Margaret Mead (Victor Gollancz, London 1956, and William Morrow, New York, p. 493) Reprinted by permission of Victor Gollancz Limited and William Morrow and Company

Coquille Jim's Dream: 'The 1870 Ghost Dance' by Cora du Bois (*Anthropological Records,* University of California Press 1939, vol. 3, p. 35)

Wovoka's Message, Short Bull and *The Rituals of the Ghost Dance:* These texts have been selected and slightly abridged from 'The Ghost Dance Religion and The Sioux Outbreak of 1890' by James Mooney (Fourteenth Annual Report of the Bureau of Ethnology, to the Smithsonian Institute 1892–93, Washington 1896, pp. 781, 788–9, 797–8)

The Starvation of the Xhosas: abridged from *Sparks from the Border Anvil* by A. W. Burton (Provincial Publishing Company, King William's Town 1950, pp. 89–90)

The Hau-hau Movement: slightly adapted from *The Revolt in New Zealand* by W. Fox (London 1865, pp. 128–9)

The Goddess Djewmé: slightly adapted from 'A Mamberamo Cargo Cult' by G. Oosterwal (*Ethnology,* vol. 2, pp. 4 and 7)

Battiste Good's Vision: The Picture Writing of the American Indians by G. Mallery (Tenth Annual Report of the Bureau of Ethnology, to the Smithsonian Institute 1888–9, Washington 1893, pp. 289–90)

Ashnithlai: 'The Feather Cult of Middle Columbia' by Cora du Bois (*General Series in Anthropology* 1938, vol. 7, p. 18)

Tail Feather Woman: slightly abridged from *Menomini Powwow* by J. S. Slotkin (Milwaukee Public Museum Publication in Anthropology 1954, no. 4, pp. 17–19) Reprinted by permission of the author and the Milwaukee Public Museum Press

The Great Snake Mumbo: slightly adapted from 'The Cult of Mumbo in Central and Southern Kavirondo by Nyangueso (pseud) (Journal of the East African and Ugandan Natural History Society 1930, nos 38 and 39, pp. 13–17)

The Rastafarians: slightly adapted from the field notes of Joan Wescott

Kelevi and the Roses of Life: abridged and slightly adapted from 'A New Religious Cult in Fiji' by A. C. Cato (*Oceania* 1947–48, vol. 17, no. 2, pp. 147, 153–6)

The Road to the Land of the Dead: slightly abridged from *Menomini Powwow* by J. S. Slotkin (Milwaukee Public Museum Publications in Anthropology 1954, no. 4, pp. 24–5) Reprinted by permission of the author and the Milwaukee Public Museum

The Yakan Water Cult: selected from 'The Yakan Water Cult' by John Middleton (*Journal of the Royal Anthropological Institute* 1963, pp. 80–108) Reprinted by courtesy of the Royal Anthropological Institute of Great Britain and Ireland and the author

Abel and Hellelujah: selected and slightly adapted from 'The Birth of a Religion' by Audrey Butt (*Journal of the Royal Anthropological Institute* 1960, no. 90, part 2, pp. 74–7) Reprinted by courtesy of the Royal Anthropological Institute of Great Britain and Ireland and the author

The God Peyote: slightly abridged from *The Diabolical Root* by Vincenzo Petrullo (University of Pennsylvania Press, Philadelphia 1934, pp. 34–7)

We are All Strangers Here: arranged by Ronald M. Berndt from 'An Oenpelli Dialogue: Culture Contact' by C. H. and R. M. Berndt (*Oceania* 1951, vol. 22, no. 1, pp. 24–52)

BIBLIOGRAPHY

Anderson, E. *Messianic Popular Movements in the Lower Congo* (Uppsala, 1958)

Attenborough, David *The Cargo Cult and the Great God Frum*, (Sunday Times, London, 24 April 1960, p. 5)

Balandier, G. *Sociologie de l' Afrique Noire* (Paris, 1955)

Bankes, George *African Carvings* (Royal Pavilion, Art Gallery and Museums, Brighton 1975)

Barrett, Leonard E. *The Rastafarians* (Heinemann for Sangster's Bookstores Ltd, Kingston 1977)

Beier, Ulli *African Mud Sculpture* (Cambridge University Press, Cambridge 1968)
Contemporary Art in Africa (Pall Mall Press, 1968)

Burland, Cotti *The Exotic White Man* (Thames & Hudson, London 1959)

Burridge, K. O. L. *Mambu: A Melanesian Millennium* (Methuen, London 1960)
New Heaven New Earth (Blackwell, Oxford 1969)

Canetti, Elias *Crowds and Power* (Victor Gollancz; London 1962; Seabury Press, New York 1977)

Cochrane, Glynn *Big Men and Cargo Cults* (Clarendon Press, Oxford 1970)

Coe, Ralph T. *Sacred Circles. 200 Years of North American Indian Art* (Arts Council of Great Britain, 1977)

Cole, Herbert 'Mbari is a Dance', *African Arts* (University of California Publication Spring, Summer and Fall 1969)

Davenport, William and Coker, Gulbun 'The Moro Movement of Guadalcanal, British Solomon Islands Protectorate' (*Journal of the Polynesian Society*, vol. 76, 1967, pp. 123-75)

Deacon, A. Bernard *Malekula: a Vanishing People in the New Hebrides* (Routledge & Kegan Paul, London 1934)

Driberg, J. H. 'Yakan' (*Journal of the Royal Anthropological Institute of Great Britain and Ireland* 61, July–December 1931, pp. 413-20)

Du Bois, Cora *The Feather Cult of the Middle Columbia* (George Banta, Menasha, Wisc., 1938)
'The 1870 Ghost Dance' (*Anthropological Records* 3, I, University of California Press, Berkeley 1939)

Farb, Peter *Man's Rise to Civilization* (Secker & Warburg, London 1969)

Greenwood, William 'The Upraised Hand, or the Spiritual Significance of the Rise of the Ringatu Faith' (*The Journal of the Polynesian Society*, 51, I, March 1942, pp. i–vi, 1–81)

Guiart, Jean *The Arts of the South Pacific* trans. Anthony Christie (Thames & Hudson 1973; Edition Gallimard, Paris 1963)

Lanternari, Vittorio *The Religions of the Oppressed; A Study of Modern Messianic Cults* trans. Lisa Sergio (MacGibbon and Kee, London 1963; Alfred Knopf, New York)

Lawrence, Peter *Road Belong Cargo: A Study of the Cargo Movement in the Southern Madang District, New Guinea* (Manchester University Press, Manchester 1964; Humanities Press, New York)

Lesser, Alexander *The Pawnee Ghost Dance Hand Game: A Study in Cultural Change* (Columbia University Press, New York 1933)

Lips, Julius *The Savage Hits Back* (Lovat Dickson Ltd, London 1937)

Mallery, Garrick *Picture-Writing of the American Indians* (Smithsonian Bureau of American Ethnology, Tenth Annual Report 1888–89)

Man, E. H. 'The Nicobar Islands' (*The Royal Anthropological Institute of Great Britain and Ireland*, 1933)

Mead, Margaret *New Lives for Old* (Victor Gollancz, London 1963; William Morrow, New York 1956)

Middleton, John 'Lugbara Religion' (*International African Institute,* 1960)

Mooney, James *The Ghost Dance Religion and the Sioux Outbreak of 1890* (Fourteenth Annual Report of the Bureau of Ethnology to the Secretary of the Smithsonian Institute, Government Printing Office, Washington 1896)

Neihardt, John G. (Ed.) *Black Elk Speaks* (University of Nebraska Press, Lincoln, Neb. 1961; Sphere Books, London 1974)

Peterson, Harold (Ed.) *I Wear the Morning Star* (Minneapolis Institute of the Arts Publication 1976)

Petrullo, Vincenzo *The Diabolical Root. A Study of Peyotism, the new Indian Religion among the Delawares* (University of Pennsylvania Press, Philadelphia 1934)

Rothenberg, Jerome *Technicians of the Sacred* (Doubleday and Co. Inc., New York 1968)

Roux, Edward *Time Longer then Rope* (Victor Gollancz, London 1945; University of Wisconsin Press, Madison 1964)

Sundkler, B. G. M. *Bantu Prophets in South Africa* (London 1948)

Thrupp, Sylvia L. (Ed.) *Millennial Dreams in Action: Essays in Comparative Study* (Comparative Studies in Society and History Supplement 2, Mouton, The Hague; Humanities Press, New York 1962)

Vinnecombe Carter, Patricia *The People of the Eland* (University of Natal Press 1976)

Wallis, W. D. *Messiahs: Their Role in Civilization* (Washington 1943)

Willett, Frank *African Art* (Thames & Hudson, London 1970; OUP, New York 1977)

Wilson, Bryan R. *Magic and the Millenium* (Paladin, London 1975; Harper & Row, New York 1973)

INDEX

Numbers in italics refer to illustrations
'Abel and Hallelujah' 176–7
Abeokuta, Nigeria *114*
Aborigines, Australian 25, 88, *95*, *182–3*
  Booandik 33–4
  Gunwinggu 181–3
  Murngin 91, 94–7
  Northern Territory 68, *69*, 70, 115–16
Adam and Eve 87–8, 97–8, 107
Adam and Eve panel (Olatunde) *96*
'Adam and Riva in Devil-Devil Country' 115–16
Admiralty Islands 62, 64–5, 123–4
aeroplanes 29, 46, 47, 49, 65, 69, 82, 85
Akawaio, Guyana 176–7
Ala (Ibo earth goddess) *12*
Alaska 31–3
'All People Come from the Same Place' 112–13
Amazula, South Africa 106, 108–9
Ambo 35, 37
Ambrose, Captain, D.C. *26*
ancestors, ancestor worship 17–18, 42, 56, 57, 73–4, 76–7, 78–80, 95, 119–49
Arapaho Indians 130, 134, 136, 137
  Ghost Dances *24*, *126*, 131, *138*
Arctic Canada 104–5
Arnhem Land *69*, 94–7, *181–3*
'The Arrival of the White Men' 26–7
'Ashnithlai' 156–7

bamboo poles, carved (from New Caledonia) *14*, *21*, *30*, *40*, *63*, *125*
bankiboro snake 109
Bantu 97–8
  Fang 58, 60, 62
  Meru 112–13
Bas, Rastafarian prophet *165*
Ba-Teke people *38*
'Battiste Good's Vision' 152–5
'Battle of the Hundred Slain' (1866), 44, *44*
Battle of Wounded Knee (1890) 130
Bekukua dance 60
Belenbangara, Chief 45–6
'Berebi and the Shivering Poison' 73–4, 76–7
Berndt, Catherine H. 181
Bethonas 58
Biafra *12*, 88
'Bichiwung goes to Engiland' 53, 70–3, 176
'The Big Bird Comes' 29
'Big-House-Ship' 33–4
Bittremieux, P. Leo *19*
Black Elk 42, 44–5, 151, *158*
Booandik Aborigines 33–4
  rock paintings, *31*, *107*, *122*

Callaway, Rev. 106
cargo cults 64, 74, 77–80, *81*, 84, *166*
Cartier, Jacques 91
cave painting, Aboriginal *69*
cemetery art, western *108*
Cheyenne Indians 129, 130, 134, *138*

'Christ on the Cross' (Papuan carving) *150*
Chuckchi Eskimos *103*
Cleveland, Rev. 155
Cold Bokkeveld rock paintings *31*, *122*
Comanche Indians 177, 178
'The Coming of the Wasichu' 42, 44–5
Congo *15*
  carved wooden stick from *20*
  Passport to Heaven from *175*
  portrait of missionary from *111*
'Coquille Jim's Dream' 124, 126–9
Crow Indians 134, *135*
custom house, Guadalcanal *167*

Dakota Indians *44*, 132, *133*, 134, 136, 152, 155–6, *158*
Dancing Rite 158–9
dancing spirits of rain and fertility 117
'The Day of the Crocodiles' 58, 60, 62
Deacon, Bernard *56*, 101–2
Delaware Indians 177–80
Deuse, god the creator 47, *55*, 74–5
Djēwmé, goddess 146–9
Dream dance, Paiute 124, 126, 128
Drum religion 158–9, *160*, 161, 170

Eastern Highlanders, Papua New Guinea 29, 39–42, 73
Edward VII, King, portrait of *15*
epidemics, illnesses 101–2, 120, 172–3
Eskimos:
  Chuckchi, *103*
  Netsilik, 91, 104–5

Fang 58, 60, 62
Fante military shrine *153*
Fiji, Fijians 168–70
Finnegan, Ruth 109
Fore people 73–4, 76–7
Frum, John 79, *84*
funerary statue, West African *121*

Garvey, Marcus, 163
Gehe people 45
ghosts, ghost-spirits 45, 46, 77, 79–80, 92
Ghost Dance religion/movement 25, 126–7, *128*, 129, 130, 132, 134
  Arapaho, *24*, *126*, 131, *138*
  buckskin pictograph, *138*
  painted buckskin dress, *131*
  painted shield, *135*
  rituals, 136–9, *139*
Ghost Wind 74, 76
'Gluscap (The Man Made First) and Hadam' 91–2, 94
'The God Peyote' 177–80
'The Goddess Djēwmé' 146–9
'The Great Snake Mumbo' 161–3
Guadalcanal, custom house on *167*
Gunwinggu Aborigines 181–3

Guyana, South America:
  Akawaio 176–7
  Makusi 70–3

Haddon, A.C. *52*
Hagen people 46–9
Haida Indians:
  argillite carving of missionaries *93*
  mask of sailor *90*
  portrait bust of sailor *32*
Haile Selassie 163, 166
Haimbili, King 35, 37
Hallelujah religion 70–3, 176–7
Hau-hau Movement (1890) 25, 142–5
'Houses Bulging with Cargo' 77–80
'How Snakes Crawl Inside the Women' 41–2

Ibibio memorial to deceased chief *108*
'The Indian Who Danced' 116–17

Jamaica, Rastafarians in 163–6
Johnny-The-Thunderer-Comes-With-Noise-Of-Thunder 159, 170

Kainantu 40, 41, 74
Kamano 40, 42
'Kanu and the Book' 109–10, 112
Keiginama (spirits of the dead) 76
'Kelevi and the Roses of Life' 268–70
Kenya:
  Luo and Kisii 161–3
  Meru Bantu 112–13
Kickapoo Indians *179*
Kisii 161–3
Klikitat Indians 34–5, 156–7
Kuanyama 35, 37, 39

'La Pérouse at Lituya Bay' 31–3
Lakota Sioux Indians 42, 44–45
'The Landing of Alvaro de Mendana' 45–6
Leahy, Michael and Dan 46, 47, 49
Limba, 88, 109–10, 112
Lituya Bay 31–3
Luba *15*
Lugbara 172–4
Luo 161–3

'Macassar White Man and Dog' 94–7
Madang area, Papua New Guinea 82
magic shield *47*
Makusi 70–3, 176
Malekula islanders *56*, 101–2, 104
Mamberamo 146–9
'Mambu goes to Australia' 54, 56–8
Man, E.H. *91*
'The Man who saw them First' 39–40
Mandume, King 37
Manus Islanders 62, 64–5, 123–4
Maoris, New Zealand 25, 123, 142–5
Maori Wars (1863–65) 143, 145